Glo

Human Security in the Global Economy

Series editor: Professor Caroline Thomas (Southampton University).

Also available

The Politics of Human Rights
A Global Perspective
Tony Evans

Global Governance, Development and Human Security

The Challenge of Poverty and Inequality

Caroline Thomas

Pluto Press

LONDON • STERLING, VIRGINIA

Arawak

KINGSTON JAMAICA

First published 2000 by Pluto Press
345 Archway Road, London N6 5AA
and 22883 Quicksilver Drive,
Sterling, VA 20166–2012, USA

www.plutobooks.com

and Arawak publications
17 Kensington Crescent, Kingston 5, Jamaica

British Library Cataloguing in Publication Data
A catalogue record for this book is available from the British Library

Library of Congress Cataloging in Publication Data
Thomas, Caroline, 1959–
  Global governance, development and human security : the challenge
of poverty and inequality / Caroline Thomas.
      p. cm.—(Human security in the global economy)
Includes bibliographical references and index.
  ISBN 0–7453–1426–0
  1. Poverty. 2. Economic security. 3. Economic development—Social
aspects. 4. Security, International—Social aspects. I. Title. II. Series.
  HC79.P6 T52 2001
  303.44—dc21   00–009390

National Library of Jamaica Cataloguing in Publication Data
Thomas, Caroline
  Global governance, development and human security : the challenge
of poverty and inequality / Caroline Thomas
      p. ; cm.—(Human security in the global economy)
  1. Social sciences 2. Economics—Sociological aspects 3. Poverty
I. Title II. Series
  339.46—dc20

ISBN 0 7453 1426 0 hardback (Pluto Press)
ISBN 0 7453 1421 X paperback (Pluto Press)
ISBN 976 95047 1 8 (Arawak publications)

09   08   07   06   05   04   03   02   01   00
10   9   8   7   6   5   4   3   2   1

Designed and produced for Pluto Press by Chase Production Services
Typeset by Stanford DTP Services, Northampton
Printed in the European Union by TJ International, Padstow

Contents

Acknowledgements   vii

Preface: Human Security in a Global Economy   xi

List of Boxes and Tables   xiii

List of Acronyms and Abbreviations   xiv

Part One:
The Human Security Challenge

1. Setting the Scene   3

2. Mapping Inequality   23

3. Ideas About Development   34

Part Two:
Global Development Practice in the 1980s and 1990s

4. The Reform of National Economies   55

5. Liberalisation of Trade, Finance and Investment   69

Part Three:
**Development Pathways for Human Security in
the Twenty-first Century**

6. The Reformist Pathway for the Twenty-first Century   93

7. Towards an Alternative Pathway for the Twenty-first
   Century   110

References and Bibliography   128

Index   143

Acknowledgements

I would like to thank an extended network of family, friends and colleagues near and far who continue to provide encouragement and support. Roger van Zwanenberg of Pluto Press recognised the importance of the human security approach and offered the opportunity to develop a book series dedicated to this. He had faith in me to deliver a contribution to start off the series, and I thank him for that. The Politics Department in Southampton provides a stimulating and supportive environment in which to work. To Steve Thomas, Amanda Burrell, Lynda Smith, Sue Cavanagh, Sandi Harvey, Patricia Glasspool, Helle Amin and my mother, I offer a special thank you. Finally, my deep gratitude and affection to Heloise and Martin Weber, for their friendship, support and intellectual understanding, and to Heloise, for blessing me with her terrific smile.

Dedication

For Steve and Alia, who put up with me being here but not there.

Preface: Human Security in a Global Economy

The idea for this series grew out of a panel on human security at the British International Studies Association (BISA) conference in December 1998. Panellists expressed concern at the silence of the International Relations discipline in the face of growing inequality and widespread poverty that characterised the era of neoliberal development. The uneven distribution of the benefits of the globalisation process, and the general failure of that process to attend to the human security of the majority of humanity, were noted. There was a desire to remove the intellectual blinkers arising from an emphasis on a state-level analysis and to put people first.

The series is concerned with the area of convergence between International Relations and Development Studies. In contrast to most International Relations series, which take the state as the central unit of analysis, this series gives primacy to human beings and their complex social, political, economic and cultural relations. Importantly, the concept of human security pursued here differs fundamentally from competitive, possessive notions of security of the individual conceived in the currently fashionable neoliberal sense. Rather, human security describes a condition of existence in which basic material needs are met and in which human dignity, including meaningful participation in the life of the community, can be met. Thus, while material sufficiency lies at the core of human security, in addition the concept encompasses non-material dimensions to form a qualitative whole. Human security is oriented towards an active and substantive notion of democracy, and is directly engaged with discussions of democracy at all levels, from the local to the global.

The series investigates the causes of human insecurity and the pursuit of human security. For the majority of humankind, human security is pursued as part of a collective, most commonly the household, sometimes the community defined along other lines such as religion, caste, ethnicity or gender, or a combination of these. States play a critical role in the achievement of human security; they have the authority and the responsibility to attend to the human security needs of citizens. State–society relations are up for scrutiny, as fundamental questions arise concerning state capacity, state legitimacy and state collapse. Global processes may impact on, even jeopardise human security; these processes and the global governance structures that drive them need investigation. Regional organisations and global governance institutions set and implement the global development agenda and the global security agenda. Private transnational banks and transnational corporations exert a huge influence. Indeed the development of the global economy requires us to consider humanity embedded not simply within discrete territorial states, but within a global social structure: the capitalist world economy that has been developing since the sixteenth century. The aim is the exposure of policies which undermine the fulfilment of human security and the articulation of processes, policies and practices which support it.

List of Boxes and Tables

Boxes

1.1 Global deprivation, 1997   12
1.2 Major agencies of global economic governance,
     mid-1990s   18
2.1 Global polarisation at the end of the twentieth century   24
3.1 Free market beliefs   40
3.2 Underlying assumptions of neoclassical economics   41
6.1 The Nine Principles: UN Secretary-General Kofi
     Annan's Global Compact for the New Century   106
7.1 The Fairtrade Foundation's Charter   117
7.2 Fairtrade Foundation's basic principles of Fairtrade
     coffee   118

Tables

1.1 Global economic governance, 1997: the G7 and
     the G77   19
1.2 Formal distribution of voting power in the IMF, 2000   19
2.1 Changing income ratios   24
2.2 Concentration of global income, resources and wealth,
     1999   25
2.3 The ultra-rich, by origin, 1997   28
2.4 Total value of mergers and acquisitions, 1988 and
     1998   32
2.5 Top ten mergers, 1998   33
3.1 The orthodox versus the alternative view of
     development   38
5.1 Top corporations' sales and countries' GDP, 1997   85
5.2 Infrastructure privatisations in developing countries,
     1988–95   89
7.1 The world's priorities?   127

List of Acronyms and Abbreviations

ADB	African Development Bank
AFTA	ASEAN Free Trade Area
AIDS	acquired immunodeficiency syndrome
AMF	Asian Monetary Fund
APEC	Asia Pacific Economic Cooperation
AsDB	Asian Development Bank
ASEAN	Association of South East Asian Nations
BIS	Bank for International Settlements
BP	British Petroleum
CAFOD	Catholic Fund for Overseas Development
CERDS	Charter of Rights and Duties of States
CGAP	Consultative Group to Assist the Poorest
CIS	Commonwealth of Independent States
DAC	Development Assistance Committee (of the OECD)
EBNSC	European Business Network for Social Cohesion
EBRD	European Bank for Reconstruction and Development
ECAs	export credit agencies
ECLAC	United Nations Economic Commission for Latin America and the Caribbean
ESA	Environmental Side Agreement
ESAF	Enhanced Structural Adjustment Facility
ESCAP	United Nations Economic and Social Commission for Asia and the Pacific
ESF	Emergency Social Fund
EU	European Union
EURODAD	European Network on Debt and Development
FDI	foreign direct investment
FOE–US	Friends of the Earth – United States
G8	Group of 8
G10	Group of 10
G20	Group of 20
G7	Group of 7 leading industrial states
G77	Group of 77 least developed states
GATT	General Agreement on Tariffs and Trade
GDOs	grassroots development organisations

GDP	gross domestic product
GNP	gross domestic product
HDI	Human Development Index
HIPC	Heavily Indebted Poor Countries
HIV	human immunodeficiency virus
ICC	International Chamber of Commerce
ICFTU	International Confederation of Free Trade Unions
IFC	International Finance Corporation
IFIs	international financial institutions
ILO	International Labour Organisation
IMF	International Monetary Fund
IOSCO	International Organisation for Securities Commissions
ISO	International Organisation for Standardisation
IUCN	International Union for the Conservation of Nature
LTCM	Long Term Capital Management (hedge fund)
MAI	Multilateral Agreement on Investment
MIGA	Multilateral Investment Guarantee Agency
NAAEC	North American Agreement on Environmental Cooperation
NAALC	North American Agreement on Labour Co-operation
NAFTA	North American Free Trade Agreement
NGO	non-governmental organisation
NIEO	New International Economic Order
OAU	Organization of African Unity
ODA	official development assistance
ODI	Overseas Development Institute
OECD	Organization for Economic Co-operation and Development
PAMSCAD	Programme of Actions to Mitigate the Social Costs of Adjustment
PRGF	Poverty Relief and Growth Facility
RFSTNRP	Research Foundation for Science, Technology and National Resource Policy (India)
SADC	Southern African Development Community
SAP	structural adjustment programme
SEATINI	Southern and Eastern African Trade Information and Negotiations Initiative
TINA	'There is no alternative'
TNBs	transnational banks
TNCs	transnational corporations
TRIMs	trade-related investment measures
TRIPs	trade-related aspects of intellectual property rights

TUAC	Trade Union Advisory Committee to the OECD
UN	United Nations
UNCED	United Nations Conference on Environment and Development
UNCTAD	United Nations Conference on Trade and Development
UNCTC	United Nations Center on Transnational Corporations
UNDP	United Nations Development Programme
UNEP	United Nations Environment Programme
UNICEF	United Nations Children's Fund
UNRATTI	United Nations Regulatory Agency for Transnational Trade and Investment
UNU/WIDER	United Nations University/World Institute for Development Economics Research
WBCSD	World Business Council on Sustainable Development
WCED	World Commission on Environment and Development
WES	World Economic Summit
WHO	World Health Organization
WIPO	World Intellectual Property Organization
WTO	World Trade Organization
WWF	World Wide Fund for Nature

PART ONE

The Human Security Challenge

CHAPTER 1

Setting the Scene

> Poverty is the ultimate systemic threat facing humanity. The widening gaps between rich and poor nations ... are ... potentially socially explosive...If the poor are left hopeless, poverty will undermine societies through confrontation, violence and civil disorder. (Michel Camdessus, Managing Director of the International Monetary Fund (IMF), speaking at the United Nations Conference on Trade and Development (UNCTAD) X meeting in Bangkok, February 2000)

> In a world awash with resources, wealth and technology, global poverty is certainly not the product of bad luck. (Wilkin, 2000)

Pervasive poverty and deepening inequality are distinctive features of the contemporary global social landscape. Powerful global governance institutions are awakening to these fault-lines as potential threats to the global order. On 10 January 2000, the United Nations Security Council, the most important global body dedicated to tackling security issues, met to discuss the challenge of HIV/AIDS in Africa. The focus of the meeting was far removed from the traditional concerns of the Security Council, which were mainly military threats to regional and global order. This is indicative of a widening of the global security agenda to encompass non-traditional matters, such as health, environment and poverty issues.

Moreover, for the first time, a World Bank president was invited to address the Security Council. World Bank President James Wolfensohn, in his speech to the meeting, remarked that 'If we want to prevent violent conflict, we need a comprehensive, equitable, and inclusive approach to development.' Development is moving to the centre stage of the global political agenda, largely on account of the realisation of current leaders of global governance agencies that development and security are intimately linked. HIV/AIDS, a matter that previously had been considered within the UN system as a health issue, is evolving into a global security concern.

The convergence of the development and security agendas is the concern of this book. The focus is selected not in response to the increased level of interest of leaders of global governance institutions, but rather in recognition of the ancient and enduring concerns of humanity. For the overwhelming majority of people on this planet, human security is their primary concern. As Nelson Mandela remarked on the dawn of the new millennium, ordinary people want 'the simple opportunity to live a decent life, to have a proper shelter and food to eat, to be able to care for their children and to live with dignity, to have good education for their charges, their health needs cared for and to have access to paid employment' (cited by Camdessus, 2000c).

Human insecurity is not some inevitable occurrence. Of course, natural catastrophes such as drought undermine human security, but even within a single locality they do not undermine everyone's security equally. Rather, human insecurity results directly from existing power structures that determine who enjoys the entitlement to security and who does not. Such structures can be identified at several levels, ranging from the global, through the regional, the state and finally the local level. For a growing number of people, the failure of the state and of the global market to facilitate the enjoyment of human security has resulted in their pursuit of human security through the informal sector, beyond the reach of the formal institutions of the state. The purpose of this book is to contribute a few pieces of this complex, multi-dimensional jigsaw, by broadening awareness of the global-level structures which impact on human security and by considering what might be done to promote improvements.

This book is concerned directly with the global development agenda and the material polarisation which is unfolding in the wake of its application. The growth of material inequality is evident between states, within states, and also between private corporations. This impacts directly on the contemporary human experience of security, and on future prospects for enhancing human security.

Regarding future prospects for human security, there is a very simple but hugely important question as to whether the mechanisms in place to tackle poverty and to promote wider development are adequate to the task. In 1995, the UN set a target of a 50 per cent reduction in the number of people existing in absolute poverty by 2015. This outcome is to be delivered not by any redistributive mechanism, but rather the application of the particular neoliberal model of development promoted in the 1980s and 1990s by global governance institutions. This model places its faith in the market rather than the state, and focuses on export-led growth based on free capital mobility. The model represents a significant departure from the earlier embedded liberalism of the post-Second World War period. It is even further removed from a critical alternative model of development that places basic needs at its centre.

The neoliberal model requires high and sustained growth to achieve the UN's target for poverty reduction. African economies, for example, would need to grow at an estimated 7 per cent a year on average to reach the target by 2015 (Amoako, 1999). Yet even if such growth is sustained in Africa and elsewhere, can we be confident that it will translate into a 50 per cent reduction in the absolute poor? How will the benefits and the costs be distributed? Moreover, beyond this initial goal, can it enhance significantly the human security of the rest of humanity? If not, does the solution lie in reform of the existing model, or transformation of it? These questions matter. The scope, depth and speed of the changes that have been, and continue to be, introduced in development policy are breathtaking. Their legitimacy is open to question, and the futures of billions will be deeply affected by them.

In this introductory chapter, the scene is set for the rest of the book. The chapter begins with a discussion of human security, arguing that material sufficiency lies at its core. Hence the problems of poverty and of deepening inequality are central, and the unfolding of these problems in the 1980s and 1990s is highlighted. This is followed by a brief overview of the neoliberal vision that has dominated the global development policy agenda whilst these problems have deepened. The policy has been developed and implemented by a range of global governance institutions. The idea and the institutions of global governance are examined, with a view to establishing in whose interest global governance may be operating. The chapter ends with a synopsis of the contents of the book.

The Human Security Challenge

> When we think about security, we need to think beyond battalions and borders. We need to think about human security, about winning a different war, the fight against poverty. (Wolfensohn, 2000)

Human Security

The concept of human security involves a fundamental departure from an orthodox, international relations security analysis that has the state as the exclusive primary referent object (Thomas and Wilkin, 1999; Thomas, 1999a). Instead, human beings and their complex social and economic relations are given primacy with or over states. Human security is about 'the ability to protect people as well as to safeguard states' (Heinbecker, 1999: 6). In some human security formulations, such as that of Canadian Foreign Minister Lloyd Axworthy, human needs rather than state needs are paramount. Axworthy believes this to be so in the aftermath of the Cold War as intrastate conflicts have become more prevalent than interstate conflicts. These conflicts are fought with low technology, and in contrast to the very beginning of the twentieth century, most of the casualties now – 75 per cent – are civilian (Smith, 1997: 14). Axworthy notes that women and children are disproportionately often the victims of these wars. For Axworthy, 'Human security includes security against economic privation, an acceptable quality of life, and a guarantee of fundamental human rights' (Axworthy, 1997: 184).

The concept of human security pursued in this study differs fundamentally from notions of 'security of the individual', conceived in the currently fashionable neoliberal sense. Human security is very far removed from liberal notions of competitive and possessive individualism (that is, the extension of private power and activity, based around property rights and choice in the market place). Rather, human security describes a condition of existence in which basic material needs are met, and in which human dignity, including meaningful participation in the life of the community can be realised. Such human security is indivisible; it cannot be pursued by or for one group at the expense of another (Thomas, 1999b).

Therefore, while material sufficiency lies at the core of human security, in addition the concept encompasses non-material dimensions to form a qualitative whole. In other words, material sufficiency is a necessary, but not sufficient, condition of human security which entails more than physical survival. For simplicity we can refer to these different aspects in terms of a quantitative/qualitative distinction, which broadly refers to income poverty and human poverty (see below).

The quantitative aspect refers to material sufficiency. In this context, Axworthy remarks that 'At minimum, human security requires that basic needs are met ...' (1997: 184). Therefore the pursuit of human security must have at its core the satisfaction of basic material needs of all humankind. At the most basic level, food, shelter, education and health care are essential for the survival of human beings.

The qualitative aspect of human security is about the achievement of human dignity which incorporates personal autonomy, control over one's life and unhindered participation in the life of the community. Emancipation from oppressive power structures, be they global, national or local in origin and scope, is necessary for human security. Human security is oriented towards an active and substantive notion of democracy, one that ensures the opportunity of all for participation in the decisions that affect their lives. Therefore it is engaged directly with discussions of democracy at all levels, from the local to the global.

Human security is pursued by the majority of humankind as part of a collective, most commonly the household, sometimes the village or the community defined along other criteria such as religion, ethnicity, gender or caste. Often it is pursued through a combination of these. At the global level, states have the authority and responsibility to attend to the human security needs of their citizens. Weak state–society relations mean that states often hinder rather than help the achievement of human security by all their citizens. Global governance institutions also play a crucial role. They set global development policy and set, apply and monitor the global entitlement rules. A consideration of human security in the contemporary era requires us to consider humanity embedded not simply within discrete sovereign states, but within a global social structure, the capitalist world economy that has been developing since the sixteenth century. In a way, the work of the United Nations Development Programme (UNDP) has leaned in that direction. The concept of human security as employed in this study was initially brought to the forefront of the global policy level by that particular UN agency.

The UNDP and Human Security

The late Dr Mahbub Ul Haq first drew global attention to the concept of human security in the UNDP's *Human Development Reports*. In 1994, the *Human Development Report* focused explicitly on human security. The report argued that:

> For too long, the concept of security has been shaped by the potential for conflict between states. For too long, security has been equated with threats to a country's borders. For too long, nations have sought arms to protect their security. For most people today, a feeling of insecurity arises more from worries about daily life than from the dread of a cataclysmic world event. Job security, income security, health security, environmental security, security from crime, these are the emerging concerns of human security all over the world. (UNDP, 1994: 3)

The 1994 report, by focusing on human security, sought to influence the UN's 1995 World Summit on Social Development in Copenhagen. Throughout the late 1990s, the UNDP's annual reports built on and refined this concept. In 1997, the focus was on human development, which refers not simply to the income aspects of poverty, but to poverty as a denial of choices and opportunities for living a tolerable life (UNDP, 1997: 2). Significantly, the 1997 report further disaggregated what we referred to earlier as the quantitative and qualitative dimensions of human security, making a distinction between income poverty (US$ 1 a day and below) and human poverty (illiteracy, short life expectancy, and so forth). Income poverty and human poverty are often, but not always, linked; for example in the Gulf States, people may suffer human poverty without being income poor. These two aspects tally broadly with the quantitative and qualitative aspects of human security discussed above.

The UNDP played a crucial agenda-setting role at an early stage with its focus on human security. It was noted earlier that development and human security are receiving more attention now from the key global governance institutions such as the IMF and World Bank, partly because poverty and inequality are increasingly considered to be national, regional and global security threats. Indeed, there seems to be a correlation between the level of entitlement to human security and the propensity for conflict, defined not in orthodox interstate terms but in the wider sense to include the most frequent form of warfare, intrastate. Over the period 1990–95, 57 per cent of countries experiencing war were ranked low on the UNDP's Human Development Index, while only 14 per cent were ranked high, and 34 per cent were ranked medium (Smith, 1997: 48). There may be a causal relationship between lack of material entitlement, health and education, and war.

One explanation of this tragic outcome may be that fundamental economic and social structures allow a privileged global and national elite to control a disproportionate share of available resources. This impacts directly on security:

> When a privileged elite defends its too large share of too few resources, the link is created between poverty, inequality and the abuse of human rights. The denial of basic freedoms – to organise, to express yourself, to vote, to disagree – forces people to choose between accepting gross injustice and securing a fairer share by violent means. As conflict unfolds, the political leaders that emerge often find that the easiest way of mobilising support is on an ethnic basis. Thus do the various causes of conflict weave in and out. War will only end if, and when, and where its causes are removed. (Smith, 1997: 15)

Smith elucidates the poverty, inequality and security link clearly. With one-sixth of the world's population receiving 80 per cent of global income, and 57 per cent of the global population consuming only 6 per cent of global income, the concerns about poverty and security expressed earlier by Camdessus and Wolfensohn appear legitimate (*World Bank Development News*, 14 April 2000). (See Chapter 2 for more details on division of global income and resources.)

Yet it is important to remember that the issues of poverty and inequality matter to human beings in the most potent way, irrespective of whether global governance organisations categorise them as security issues. It is also worth recalling that the total number of people killed during the First and Second World Wars is estimated as having been about 30 million. Compare this figure with the number of people who currently die of hunger-related causes each year, that is, 15 million. Consequently we can say that every two years the number of people who die of hunger is roughly equivalent to the number killed in eleven years of world war (Thomas and Reader, 1997: 109).

The fundamental causes at the root of hunger, poverty and inequality must be addressed, or the achievement of human security will be impossible.

Human Security: Looking Forward

The change in the primary referent object of security from state to human being has implications both for understanding the sources of threats to security, and for elucidating strategies to increase security. Importantly the shift in focus from the rights, concerns and needs of states to those of human beings or citizens opens up the state for critical scrutiny. As state–society relations come under the spotlight fundamental questions arise, such as those about state capacity, state legitimacy and state collapse. Particular issues come to the fore, such as the use of child combatants in intrastate conflicts, and patterns of land tenure, which may help to keep people poor.

But the shift in focus to human security also highlights the importance of scrutinising global processes that may impact on, even jeopardise, security and the global governance structures which drive these processes. A proper understanding of the process of global economic integration and of the distribution of associated costs and benefits is crucial. Armed with this knowledge, an informed debate can take place on global development policy. This is already happening. We can work to reconstruct development policy in the cause of attending to the human security needs of all global citizens, particularly the poorest. Too many people are dying of hunger and disease. This is not the product of bad luck, but rather of existing structures which can be changed.

Poverty and Inequality: A Cause for Concern

Liberal-pluralists who have been influenced by the classical, neo-classical and monetarist approaches in economics, the functionalist and post-industrialist approaches in sociology and the

democratic pluralist approaches in political science adopt a
relatively compliant approach to the continuation of widespread
and severe poverty. (Townsend, 1993: 6)

At the dawn of the twenty-first century, despite fifty years of official
development policies and despite huge advances in science and
technology, inequalities between and within states are growing, and
almost a third of humanity continues to live in abject poverty (see
Thomas and Reader, 1997; Thomas, 1997a, 1999a, and also
Chapter 2). Yet in the economically advanced countries, and
amongst a significant strata in developing countries, there is at best
complacency about these issues. This can be attributed to the
widespread influence of the neoliberal political ideology (see
below). Moreover, these serious matters have received a
diminishing amount of attention from the media in the First World.

Losing Perspective, a study commissioned for the UK's leading
international aid, development and environment charities,
revealed a dramatic decline in the quantity and quality of coverage
of the developing world over the period 1989–99 (Stone, 2000).
Commenting on the report, Vidal remarks: 'The total number of
hours of factual programming on developing countries has
declined by 50 per cent; ITV has dropped its coverage by 74 per
cent; BBC2 by more than a third, Channel 4 by 56 per cent.' In
addition, the report notes that 60 per cent of all UK TV
programming about poor countries, which house 80 per cent of
the global population, are about travel and wildlife: 'BBC1 is
increasingly obsessed with soft wildlife and travel programmes and
Channel 5 has commissioned almost nothing from non-western
sources since it was set up' (Vidal, 2000: 6–7).

The author of *Losing Perspective*, Jenny Stone, argues that the
lack of coverage of developing countries is not simply due to a
question of a lack of interest on the part of the public. It has much
to do with other factors such as diminishing budgets, changes in
production culture and the advent of new technologies (Vidal,
2000). Vidal concurs with Stone that the emphasis on increasing
choice in broadcasting in the 1990s has undermined its public
service value. This is a worrying development, as the main source
of information for the British public on the rest of the world is such
broadcasting (Stone, 2000; Vidal, 2000).

While many people in developed countries may remain in
blissful ignorance, it is the case that the post-Cold War global
landscape is characterised by an intensification and reconfiguration of pre-existing economic, social and political inequalities. The
demise of the communist bloc and the associated rejection of 'real
existing socialism' as a mode of economic organisation have
provided a specific additional fillip to the reconfiguration of the

Third World: the Second World, the former communist bloc, has joined the Third World rather than the First World. This suggests that post-1989, the Third World, far from disappearing, is becoming global (Thomas, 1999a).

The dynamic of economically driven globalisation is resulting in the global reproduction of Third World problems. Growing inequality, risk and vulnerability characterise not simply the state system, but an emerging global social order. There is a North in the South, just as there is a South in the North. This is part of an historical process which has been underway for five centuries: the expansion of capitalism across the globe. Technological developments speed up this process. Individuals' life chances and the viability of households and communities are increasingly tied up with their respective positions in the global economy. James Gustave Speth of the UNDP has spoken of ways in which 'An emerging global elite, mostly urban-based and inter-connected in a variety of ways, is amassing great wealth and power, while more than half of humanity is left out' (cited in Crossette, 1996). Two-thirds of the global population seem to have gained little or nothing from the economic growth that has occurred as a result of globalisation to date. Moreover, even in the developed world, 'the lowest quartile seems to have witnessed a trickle up rather than a trickle down' (*Financial Times*, 24 December 1994).

Despite significant improvements over the 1990s in global social indicators such as adult literacy (64 per cent to 76 per cent), access to safe water (40 per cent to 72 per cent) and infant mortality rates (from 76 to 58 per 1000 live births), global deprivation continues (UNDP, 1997: 22). (See Box 1.1.)

These global social indicators of human security have declined despite the promise of the peace dividend of the late 1980s. Expectations had been raised that deprivation and material inequalities would be ameliorated, as resources freed up from the arms race would be diverted to accelerate development. This has not happened. Global military spending declined over the period 1987–94 at about 3.6 per cent per annum, yielding a cumulative dividend of US\$ 935 billion. Yet 'there has been no clear link between reduced military spending and enhanced spending on human development' (UNDP, 1994: 8). What's more, even if the hoped-for peace dividend *had* materialised, its impact would have been tempered by the constraints of the workings of the global economy. Yet the failure to deliver even on the promise of the peace dividend represents a significant indication of the lack of genuine commitment by agents of global power to work towards the achievement of human security.

The associated material challenges for the achievement of human security in the new century are immense: the reduction of

Box 1.1: Global deprivation, 1997

Health
- HIV/AIDS infections increased from less than 15 million in 1990 to more than 33 million in 1997
- 880 million people lack access to health services
- 2.6 billion lack access to sanitation
- 1.5 billion will not survive to the age of 60

Education
- Over 850 million illiterate adults
- Over 260 million children are out of school at the primary and secondary levels

Nutrition
- 840 million people are malnourished

Poverty
- 1.3 billion people live on less than US$ 1 per day
- 1 billion cannot meet basic consumption requirements

Women
- 340 million women are not expected to survive to the age 40
- A quarter to a half of all women have suffered physical abuse by an intimate partner

Children
- 160 million children are malnourished
- 250 million children are working as child labourers

Environment
- 3 million people a year die from air pollution – more than 80 per cent of them from indoor air pollution
- More than 5 million die per annum from diarrhoeal diseases caused by water contamination

Security
- 12 million people are refugees

Source: Adapted from UNDP, 1997: 22.

global poverty, the reduction of inequality between states and between human beings, and the harnessing of scientific advancement for the benefit of the majority of humankind. The rapid technological advances under way have the potential to decrease or increase existing inequalities, depending on how they are used and which rules determine the distribution of the benefits. These challenges require a fundamental shift in how we think about development and in the methods for its achievement (see Chapter 3).

Neoliberal Development

Neoliberalism is not a force like gravity, but an artificial construct. (George, 1999a)

Conceptions of development in the last two decades of the twentieth century were heavily influenced by what may be loosely termed as the 'New Right backlash'. The 1980s, and more particularly the 1990s since the demise of communism, have witnessed the near-universal mainstreaming of a particular brand of liberal ideology referred to hereafter as neoliberalism. Neoliberal ideology attributes universal legitimacy to a conception of freedom based on private power. It places a premium on individual choice in the market place. It attacks the public realm and associated ideas of collectivity and society. Neoliberal ideology presents a set of essentially local, Western norms as universal (Thomas, 1997b).

These norms have been shared and adopted by public institutions such as the IMF, the World Bank, other multilateral development banks, the World Trade Organization (WTO), and the majority of governments. This has provided an important legitimisation for the business of private lenders and transnational corporations (TNCs), whose vision and behaviour in most cases are underpinned by these norms. The neoliberal ideology has thus come to be promoted around the globe as the proper approach to development. Neoliberalism supports global economic integration and presents it as the best, the most natural and the universal path towards economic growth and therefore toward development for all humanity. Critics, on the other hand, see its expansion across the globe as hegemonic.

Global economic integration is to be promoted through the liberalisation of trade, investment and finance that will ensue alongside the reform of national economies (see Chapters 4 and 5). These policy prescriptions of a growing number of global governance institutions form a blueprint which has been marketed with the powerful language of 'There is no alternative', or TINA.

The appeal of neoliberalism lies in its promises of increasing an individual's control over, or consumption of, the products which capitalism is generating. Furthermore, its proponents have sought to legitimise it further by incorporation of the language of competing ideas and values. The terminology of sustainable development, transparency and accountability, that has been incorporated in the neoliberal development model, exemplifies this tendency. Thus, the dominant world-view is bolstered and lent false legitimacy.

This false legitimacy is clear given the discrepancy between its theoretical prescriptions and practical outcomes. In the wake of its practical application as a global development policy, we have seen a deepening of existing inequalities between and within states. Even these rising inequalities may be normatively legitimated by neoliberals. Within their vision, inequality can be seen as unproblematic. It may even be desirable, as it is expected to unleash entrepreneurial abilities that will contribute to maximising global wealth creation. Ultimately, therefore, everyone will benefit. The words of the British Prime Minister, Margaret Thatcher, are recalled here: 'It is our job to glory in inequality, and see that talents and abilities are given vent and expression for the benefit of us all' (1996: 52). Therefore this particular brand of liberalism not only increases global social divisions, but more dangerously it is validating global inequalities of life-chance, legitimising a situation where inequalities are greater than at any period in history.

We are witnessing and are part of the process whereby the ideology of dominant groups, presented as universal, is used to sanction the marginalisation and neutralisation of competing visions and values (see Chapters 3, 4 and 5). This is evident across a wide range of issues and areas, encompassing development, finance, trade, aid and economic policy generally, as well as ecology, human rights, law, and so forth. This particular brand of liberalism may not, however, be so universal as is often suggested. The global power structure favours a Western knowledge and a Western representation of events and processes (Thomas and Wilkin, 1997).

Since the process is not truly universal or comprehensive, then counter-hegemonic groups are able to continue offering alternative visions and practices (see Chapters 3 and 7). This was evident in the November–December 1999 Ministerial meeting of the WTO in Seattle. High-profile street protests by civil society groups, the rejection by developing-country governments of the agenda of the developed countries, and disagreement between developed countries themselves all contributed to the collapse of the meeting.

This eroded the façade of legitimacy and universality surrounding global governance institutions and their policies.

Global Governance: In Whose Interest?

The debate on globalisation and its effects on the poor is legitimate and necessary. No one has a monopoly on the truth. Everyone should have a voice, particularly the poor themselves. (James Wolfensohn, President of the World Bank, *World Bank Development News*, 22 February 2000)

The post-Cold War period has seen the move from a bipolar world in which the two superpowers governed separate spheres of influence, to a world in which global governance flourishes. But with what authority, and in whose interest? Who has a voice in global governance? Third World states have long been distinguished by, among other factors, their perception of themselves as vulnerable to external factors beyond their control, and in particular to decisions and policies – primarily economic – which they do not own. Do these Third World states, which now include the former Second World states within their ranks, perceive themselves as having a say in global governance? Or is someone speaking for them?

In this section on global governance, most attention is paid to the public agencies of global governance, especially the IMF, the World Bank and the WTO. The reason for this focus on public agencies is simple: they are supposed to be representing the interests of global citizens and promoting global public goods (see Box 2 for an illustration of the broad range of global economic governance institutions, and their respective memberships and remits).

However, this should not be taken to suggest the lesser importance of private groupings that operate alongside states and international institutions in the global governance fraternity. TNCs, for example, have a powerful influence on global economic agenda setting. They work with a range of private business interests through fora such as the International Chamber of Commerce (ICC) and the annual World Economic Summit (WES) at Davos. Moreover, Gill notes: 'At the heart of the global economy there is an internationalisation of authority and governance that not only involves international organisations (such as the BIS, IMF and World Bank) and transnational firms, but also private consultancies and private bond-rating agencies ...' (1995: 418).

Sinclair (1994) and Van der Pijl (1998) develop ideas about the roles of private bond-rating agencies and management consultancies respectively in global governance. Indeed Sinclair refers to these as 'private makers of global public policy' (Sinclair, 1994: 448).

Increasingly, business interests are cooperating not only with individual governments but also with international organisations (seen in Chapter 6, where UN Secretary-General Kofi Annan's Global Compact is discussed). The rise in collaboration between agencies mandated to provide public goods, with private interest-based agencies, is clearly visible. For example, even international organisations such as the UNDP increasingly seek collaboration and funding from private businesses (TRAC, 1999). This closeness between the private and public spheres raises important issues, especially about the democratic process. The work of Sharon Beder (1997) on corporate influence on environmental policy is indicative. This study, however, will focus primarily on the contributions and implications of public institutions in global governance.

Turning to public global governance, it is noteworthy that a recurrent theme on the liberal agenda is the presentation of a picture of a unified globe necessitating and legitimising a common response in terms of management. Thus in the 1980s we heard UN-inspired think tanks talk of 'Our Common Future', 'Common Security' and so forth. In the 1990s, we heard references to a number of global crises, including the environment, refugees and population, each requiring global management. Also in the 1990s we witnessed a series of UN-organised, partly privately funded, global conferences. These included the UN Conference on Environment and Development (UNCED) or Earth Summit at Rio in 1992, the World Summit on Social Development in Copenhagen in 1995, the 1995 International Conference on Population and Development in Cairo, the 1995 World Conference on Women in Beijing, the 1996 Human Settlements Conference in Istanbul, and, in the same year, the Rome Food Summit.

The inclusive language of such conferences, and their associated declarations, raises some important questions. Whose globe are we talking about? Who is to manage it? With what authority? In whose interest? Global management assumes a common under-standing of a particular problem and agreement about how it is to be addressed. These global conferences have undoubtedly played an important and positive role in raising awareness of pressing problems, and have helped to create the space in which debate can occur. Yet the debate has been neatly circumscribed. These conferences have lent legitimacy to a broad neoliberal framework for understanding development, and thus they have a direct bearing on human security. The liberal ideology espoused by powerful states and institutions, and accepted by the majority of governments, has offered a blueprint for global development. This model of development, with its associated methods and objectives, is assumed to be in the interest of all humanity, and it is assumed to have unquestionable authority, as it is presented as common sense (see Chapter 3).

Global governance is increasingly reflected in a conscious coordination of policies between the IMF, the World Bank, other regional multilateral development banks, the WTO and a growing number of other arms of the UN system. Recently it has been seen in aspects of the work of the UNDP and the United Nations Conference on Trade and Development (UNCTAD). The most recent of all these policy coordinations is evident in the integration of the International Labour Organisation (ILO). To different degrees and in different ways, these key institutions have been adapting their general orientation, and their respective institutional structures and policies, to facilitate movement towards a world in which for capital, if not for citizens, national economic sovereignty is an anachronism.

Influence within the public institutions of global governance directly reflects the material inequality of states. Only a handful of states exert meaningful influence in institutions such as the IMF, World Bank or WTO. While the Group of 7 (G7) has been transformed into the Group of 8 (G8) with the addition of Russia, it is the case that the G7 sets the norms and rules of global economic policy. As Sachs points out: 'The G7 countries, plus the rest of the European Union, represent a mere 14 per cent of the world's population. Yet these countries have 56 per cent of the votes in the IMF Executive Board ... The rest of the world is called upon to support G7 declarations, not to meet for joint problem solving' (1998: 2).

From where does the G7 derive the authority and legitimacy to do so? Particularly, given that the G7 is not very representative in terms of global population or indeed number of states (see Table 1.1). This is striking when compared with the Group of 77 (G77).

In this context, it is interesting to ponder for a moment on the source of democratic legitimacy of the IMF and the World Bank. As key institutions pushing the neoliberal development model that favours the private rather than the public sector, *they* are not models of democratic representation, as evidenced in Table 1.2.

The thoughts of the former Managing Director of the IMF on this matter are interesting and revealing. Just prior to leaving his post, Michel Camdessus was asked during a videoconference with journalists in three African countries whether he felt the IMF was in the hands of the big powers. His answer is quoted here at length:

Box 1.2: Major agencies of global economic governance

BIS Bank for International Settlements. Established in 1930 with headquarters in Basle. Membership of 40 central banks. Monitors monetary policies and financial flows. The Basle committee on Banking Supervision, formed through the BIS in 1974, has spearheaded efforts at multilateral regulation of global banking.

G7 Group of 7. Established in 1975 as the G5 (France, Germany, Japan, UK and USA) and subsequently expanded to include Canada and Italy. The G7 conducts semi-formal collaboration of world economic problems. Government leaders meets in annual G7 Summits, while finance ministers and/or their leading officials periodically hold other consultations.

GATT General Agreement on Tariffs and Trade. Established in 1947 with offices in Geneva. Membership had reached 122 stated when it was absorbed into the WTO in 1995. The GATT co-ordinated eight 'rounds' of multilateral negotiations to reduce state restrictions on cross-border merchandise trade.

IMF International Monetary Fund. Established in 1945 with headquarters in Washington DC. Membership of 182 states. The IMF oversees short-term cross-border money flows and foreign exchange questions. Since 1979 it has also formulated stabilisation and systemic transformation policies for states suffering chronic difficulties with transborder debt or transitions from communist central planning.

IOSCO International Organisation for Securities Commissions.

Established in 1984 with headquarters in Montreal. Membership of 115 official securities regulators and (non-voting) trade associations from 69 countries. The IOSCO develops frameworks for transborder supervision of securities firms.

OECD Organization for Economic Co-operation and Development. Founded in 1962 with headquarters in Paris. Membership of 29 states with advanced industrial economies. Drawing on a staff of 600 professional economists, the OECD prepares advisory reports on all manner of macroeconomic questions.

UNCTAD United Nations Conference on Trade and Development. Established in 1964 with office in Geneva. Membership of 187 states. UNCTAD monitors the effects of cross-border trade on macroeconomic conditions, especially in the South. It provided a key forum in the 1970s for discussions of a New International Economic Order.

WBG World Bank Group. A collection of five agencies, first established in 1945, with head offices in Washington DC. The Group provides project loans for long-term development in poor countries. Like the IMF, the World Bank has since 1979 become heavily involved in structural adjustment programmes in the South and former East.

WTO The World Trade Organization. Established in 1995 with headquarters in Geneva. The WTO is a permanent institution to replace the provisional GATT. It has a wider agenda and greater powers of enforcement.

Source: Scholte, 1997: 431.

The IMF is in the hands of its membership. As you know each country has a voting power that is in proportion to its quota, its share of IMF capital, which is itself determined more or less by the size of a country's economy. On that basis, the United States has 17.4 per cent of the voting power. That means that the rest of the world has 82.6 per cent. If my countrymen, our friends, our brothers in Europe, were united, it would be even more, something like 30 per cent of the capital of the IMF. Nobody says that Europe is controlling the IMF, even if it's a European who is sitting in this chair.

No, depending on the issues, the decisions go in one direction or another. But it's true that the developing countries, when they sit together and they join their forces in what we call here the G-11 group, represent an extremely important part of our membership.

Table 1.1: Global economic governance, 1997: the G7 and the G77

Title	Institutional Grouping	Membership	% of World GDP	% of World Pop.
G7	Western economic powers	Canada, France, Germany, Italy, Japan, the UK, the US	64.0	11.8
G77	Developing and some transitional countries (not Russian Fed. or Poland)	143 members	16.9	76.0

Source: adapted from UNDP, 1999: 109.

Table 1.2: Formal distribution of voting power in the IMF, 2000

Country	Population in Millions	% IMF Executive vote
US	276	17.68
UK	59	5.1
Germany	82	6.19
France	59	5.1
Japan	126	6.33
Saudi Arabia	21	3.27
Total of above	623	43.67
Other Countries: c.190	c.5.4 billion	56.33

Source: Compiled from IMF data, April 2000, IMF website, and UN Population Division, *Charting the Progress of Populations, 2000* – see <www.undp.org/popin/wdtrends/chart/15/15.pdf>

The fact is that, in general, our decisions are not taken by a vote where a majority imposes its solutions on a minority ... [but] ... by consensus after a long process where people in a dialogue try to understand each other's views and see where the best solution lies. At the end of the day, all of them coincide in supporting that. (Camdessus, 2000a)

The following statement, made at the end of his answer, may vindicate critics who charge the key institutions of global governance with hegemonic behaviour: 'Frequently, the Americans suggest good solutions. After all, they are present in many parts of the world. They are familiar with international life. But it is not always the case ...'

Camdessus's remarks, while factually accurate, only illuminate part of the picture. The US is the only country in the IMF with enough votes to exercise a unilateral veto power. The very existence of this veto is itself enough to ensure that the US doesn't need frequent recourse to it. The potential veto power in itself is an effective deterrent, and can be an influential factor in effecting a predetermined outcome in the form of a 'consensus'.

It is not surprising that many countries perceive a lack of distance between IMF policy and US policy. The handling of the financial crises in the late 1990s in East Asia, Russia and Brazil further eroded the trust of developing countries in the independence of the IMF. South Korea, for example, perceives congruence between IMF and US policy agendas. It regards the US as having taken advantage of the crisis to work through the IMF to push through its pre-existing trade and investment agendas (Feldstein, 1998: 32). This criticism comes from a country perceived by many to be a traditional US ally, which is also a member of the Organization for Economic Co-operation and Development (OECD). IMF restructuring of East Asian economies has enabled First World companies to snap up East Asian companies at bargain-basement prices. In 1998, European and US companies mounted over US$ 30 billion in take-overs of Asian companies – a fourfold increase on 1997 (Bello, 1999). One commentator has described this as 'the greatest global asset swindle of all time' (Hahnel, 1999). The Asian crises have also heightened awareness of the ability of a handful of relatively new private financial actors, such as hedge funds, to exert massive leverage. They can force currency devaluation at a breathtaking pace, undermine national economic policy, erode national development and throw literally millions of people below the poverty line. Global governance does not work to restrain these actors; indeed it often seems to support them.

Another important forum for global economic governance is the OECD. In reality, this is a negotiating body for the industrialised democracies, though membership during the 1990s extended to South Korea, the Czech Republic, Hungary, Poland and Mexico. (Interestingly, Turkey was a founding member in 1961.) The overwhelming majority of developing countries do not belong to the OECD, and therefore a question arises as to its legitimacy as the negotiating forum for policies and agreements of global reach. The choice of the OECD as the negotiating forum for a Multilateral Agreement on Investment (MAI) comes to mind here (see Chapters 5 and 7).

The scepticism and cynicism of developing countries and global citizens regarding global governance is understandable. From their vantage points, global governance has all the hallmarks of being 'organised under US hegemony and the international institutional structure that conforms to the interests of, broadly speaking, the G7 core capitalist states and their corporations' (Wilkin, 2000). Democratic potential at all levels, from the local to the global, is diminished by placing key decisions over policy making in the hands of ever further removed officials and institutions. It is also reduced by the influence of private interests on the public process, referred to above.

The Structure of the Book

This book is divided into three parts. Part One sets the scene. Chapter 1 has provided an overview of the issue of global governance, development and human security in the 1980s and 1990s. Chapter 2 maps the globalisation of inequality over this period at the interstate, intrastate and private company levels, and suggests some important links between the globalisation process and this deepening inequality. In Chapter 3, ideas about development are examined, and special attention is paid to the neoliberal ideas informing the development policy that was implemented world-wide during the period of the deepening material inequalities of the 1980s and 1990s. Consideration is given to the origin and spread of these ideas, and to the articulation of alternatives. In Part Two, we continue the focus on the closing decades of the twentieth century with an examination of the evolution of development policy and practice by agents of global governance. In Chapter 4, the structural and institutional reform of national economies is explored, paying special attention to IMF/World Bank structural adjustment programmes (SAPs) and the responses of these institutions to criticisms. In Chapter 5, the policy of liberalisation is analysed. Three areas are examined: the liberalisation of trade, finance and investment. In each case, key developments in the 1980s and 1990s are outlined, plus reactions and, where appropriate, policy responses. Looking to the future, in Part Three the book considers different pathways for the pursuit of human security. Mindful of deepening of inequalities and associated human insecurity, both reformists and those of a more critical inclination are mapping paths to take us beyond the current predicament. Hence we consider the different development paths being envisaged as we enter the twenty-first century. Chapter 6 explores the reformist pathway currently in the process of articulation in global governance institutions. Chapter 7 highlights alternative ideas on the appropriate direction of development for the achievement of human security. It concludes that ultimately human security requires different developmental strategies to those currently favoured by global governance institutions.

CHAPTER 2

Mapping Inequality

> The past decade has shown increasing concentration of income,
> resources and wealth among people, corporations and countries.
> (UNDP, 1999: 3)

Deepening inequality is a defining feature of the contemporary
global landscape. This inequality can be mapped in many ways.
The standard mapping involves country classifications. This state
level is important. It reveals that Third World states, far from
disappearing, have increased numerically and in terms of
geographic spread. The picture is highly differentiated, but central
characteristics of material poverty of significant sectors of the
population, vulnerability to the workings of the global market, and
lack of meaningful influence in global governance institutions, are
shared by a growing group of states. The gap between these states
and a handful in the First World is growing across all these
indicators. Inequality is increasing (Thomas, 1999a).

Yet an exclusive focus on the interstate level hides the
increasingly global social configuration of inequality, risk and
opportunity. Maps drawn using non-state criteria may reveal
significant aspects of the pervasive inequality that characterises the
current era. It is important to note that globalisation of the Third
World can be seen in the life experiences of people, as well as in
the experiences and conditions of states. There is a First World
within Third World states, and increasingly there is a Third World
within First World states. We must be mindful of this intrastate
polarisation (see Box 2.1).

Interstate Polarisation

> No fewer than 100 countries – all developing or in transition –
> have experienced serious economic decline over the past three
> decades. As a result per capita income in these 100 countries is
> lower than it was 10, 20, even 30 years ago. (UNDP, 1998: 37)

The general pace of globalisation in the 1980s and 1990s, and the
particular trajectory of capitalist expansion, has increased
inequality and risk for a broader group of countries.

Box 2.1: Global polarisation at the end of the twentieth century

- Organization of Economic Co-operation and Development (OECD) countries, with 19 per cent of the global population, have 71 per cent of global trade in goods and services, 58 per cent of foreign direct investment and 91 per cent of all Internet users.
- The world's richest 200 people more than doubled their net worth in the four years to 1998, to more than US$ 1 trillion. The assets of the top three billionaires are more than the combined GNP of all the least developed countries and their 600 million people.
- The recent wave of mergers and acquisitions is concentrating industrial power in megacorporations – at the risk of eroding competition. By 1998 the top ten companies in pesticides controlled 85 per cent of a US$ 31 billion global market, and the top ten in telecommunications, 86 per cent of a US$ 262 billion market.
- In 1993 just ten companies accounted for 84 per cent of global research and development expenditures and controlled 95 per cent of the US patents of the past two decades. Moreover, more than 80 per cent of the patents granted in developing countries belonged to residents of industrial countries.

Source: UNDP, 1999: 3.

Table 2.1: Changing income ratios

Year	Income Ratio of 20% global population in richest countries to 20% in poorest
1960	30:1
1990	60:1
1997	74:1

Source: adapted from UNDP, 1999: 3.

The increasing income gap between the fifth of the global population living in the richest countries, and the fifth living in the poorest countries, is clear in Table 2.1. This reflects a similar trend to that experienced in the last three decades of the nineteenth century when rapid global integration was also taking place: inequality defined by income between the top and bottom states increased from 3:1 in 1820, to 7:1 in 1870, to 11:1 in 1913. (UNDP, 1999: 3). In addition to income gap, inequality is evident in other spheres, as Table 2.2 reveals.

Table 2.2: Concentration of global income, resources and wealth, 1999

	20% global population in highest-income countries	20% global population in lowest-income countries
% of world GDP	86	1
% of world export markets	82	1
% of foreign direct investment	68	1
% of world telephone lines	74	1.5

Source: adapted from UNDP, 1999: 3.

The picture of poverty is uneven between countries as well as within them. At the state level, the majority of poor people are still located in the traditional developing or 'Southern' countries, though the countries of Eastern Europe and the Commonwealth of Independent States (CIS) have experienced the greatest deterioration over the 1990s. Income poverty in the latter has spread from a small proportion to well over a third of their combined population, with 120 million people living below a poverty line of US$ 4 a day. One-third of people in developing countries – over 1.5 billion – have incomes of less than US$ 1 a day. South Asian states have the greatest number of people affected by human poverty, that is, well over 515 million. Sub-Saharan African states, by contrast, have the highest proportion of people in, and fastest growth in, human poverty. Half their inhabitants are estimated to be income-poor. It is important to recognise that even in the so-called developed countries, the proportion of the population living below the poverty line (assessed there as enjoying below half of the individual median income) is increasing, standing at 100 million at the end of the twentieth century.

It is sobering to reflect that no former Second or Third World country has joined the ranks of the First World countries in a solid sense. While a handful have significantly increased their economic power – and this is a very important achievement – this has not been matched by influence in key global governance institutions. For the majority of states, global success in massively increasing consumption is not being reflected in access to the benefits of this growth. There was a moment when the achievement of East Asian states suggested that the economic gap between First and Third World states could be closed, but recent crises have shattered that hope. GDP growth in East Asia as a whole fell from 4.3 per cent to minus 6.2 per cent in the short period 1997–98 (United Nations Information Services, 1999). The Economic and Social Commission for Asia and the Pacific (ESCAP) 1999 regional survey shows that over the same period, the percentage of population in poverty has risen dramatically, as labour market displacement has been massive. For example in Indonesia the percentage in poverty has risen from 11 per cent to over 40 per cent, and unemployment from 4.7 per cent to 21 per cent. This is particularly tragic given the unique gains that had previously been made in the region to promote growth with equity and lift millions of people out of poverty (Watkins, 1998).

The transition of Central and Eastern Europe and the CIS from centrally planned to market economies has on the whole propelled these states more towards the ranks of Third World rather than First, although some – such as Poland – are faring much better than the rest. These states have acquired the characteristics of extreme vulnerability to the workings of the global market, and the resultant deepening poverty and inequality. Output in most of them remains below pre-transition levels, and unemployment is very high and rising. The Russian economy declined by over 8 per cent in 1999. The painful process of transition has been undertaken without the cushion of public provision that had previously been in place, and, in the case of Russia, with the disadvantage of highly corrupt government officials committed to capital flight of public funds for private enrichment. The number of people living in poverty in Russia has increased from 2 million to well over 60 million over the last decade. James Wolfensohn has described this increase as 'enormous' (World Bank press briefing, 22 April 1999). By 2000, an estimated 20 per cent of the population were in poverty.

Significantly, no First World country has joined the ranks of the Third World. Yet even for First World states, the risks accompanying globalisation have been brought into sharp relief. Witness the contagion effect in financial crises, the collapse of the US hedge fund Long Term Capital Management (LTCM) in September 1998, job losses due to mergers, efficiency gains and even the withdrawal of Asian investments. Importantly, however, as we saw in Chapter 1, First World states, in contrast to Third World states, enjoy a voice in global governance.

Intrastate Polarisation

Over the last fifty years, and more particularly so over the last two decades of the twentieth century, differentiation/stratification has increased at the intrastate as well as interstate level. With a few exceptions such as the East Asian tigers, the success of states, measured in terms of GDP per capita, has not been reflected in their societies at large. In Brazil, for example, the poorest 20 per cent of the population earn just 2.5 per cent of the country's income, while the richest 20 per cent enjoy roughly two-thirds. In China, Malaysia and Thailand, all of which have enjoyed strong and sustained growth, inequality grew in the 1990s, even prior to the financial crises.

Intrastate differentiation is as true for First as for Third World countries. Since the 1980s, for example, all OECD countries except Italy and Germany experienced an increase in wage inequalities – this was worst in the UK, Sweden and the US. In the UK, the number of families below the poverty line increased by 60 per cent from the early 1980s to early 1990s (UNDP, 1999: 37). Nick Davies' shocking book, *Dark Heart* (1998), paints a portrait of the UK which few readers would recognise. Concentration of wealth, and social exclusion, seem to be part of a single global process.

The dynamic of economically driven globalisation has led to a global reproduction of Third World social problems, while at the same time aggravating socio-economic divisions within weak states. In the CIS and Eastern Europe, transition has been accompanied by the removal of basic public guarantees (Andor and Summers, 1998). Huge changes have occurred in the distribution of national wealth and income; indeed, the largest ever recorded change in the case of the Russian Federation and the CIS.

This intrastate differentiation increasingly reflects the degree of integration of various social classes and geopolitical regions within the emerging global economy. Thus for each human being, their respective position in the global economy has an enormous impact on their perception and their experience of risk, vulnerability and opportunity. Let us turn to the task of mapping categories of people in the global economy, in order to see how relative position impacts on human security.

Mapping the World's Producers

Patterns of systemic inclusion and exclusion of people can be mapped with reference to the means of economic sustenance. Cox provides a useful categorisation of the world's producers in a global economy (1999: 9). He identifies a core workforce of highly skilled people integrated into the management process. A second level of precarious workers is located where business is offered the greatest incentives in terms of lowest labour costs or environmental controls. The third level comprises the rest, that is, the expanding pool of people in the First and Third World states who are excluded from international production – the 37 million unemployed plus the low skilled in the rich countries, and the 1 billion under- or unemployed, the marginalised in the poor countries. (ILO, 1998: 1). Susan George claims that 'Radical exclusion is the order of the day' (George, 1999a).

Mapping the core
The core refers to those people who are able to take advantage of the opportunities which global economic integration presents. Within this group also sit the super-rich (see Table 2.3). The world's richest 225 people have a combined wealth equal to the annual income of 47 per cent of the world's people (UNDP, 1998: 30). The three richest people have assets exceeding the combined GDP of the 48 least developed countries. Eighty-three of these ultra-rich people, that is over a third, are non-OECD citizens.

Table 2.3: The ultra-rich, by origin, 1997

Region or country group	Distribution of 225 richest people	Combined wealth of ultra-rich (US$ billion)	Average wealth of ultra-rich (US$ billion)
OECD	143	637	4.5
Asia	43	233	5.4
Latin America and the Caribbean	22	55	2.5
Arab states	11	78	7.1
Eastern Europe and CIS	4	8	2.0
Sub-Saharan Africa	2	4	2.0
Total	225	1,015	23.5

Source: UNDP, 1998: 30.

The core of people who are already reaping the benefits of the globalisation process will be able to advantage themselves further by their ability to exploit lifelong learning opportunities, and to tap into ongoing technological advance and the related communications revolution. The highly mobile and well-paid global professional elite, composed, for example, of corporate executives and scientists, has the potential to be self-sustaining.

The UN ESCAP Survey 1999 identifies the future as Internet commerce. However, e-commerce may intensify disparities between rich and poor. Out of the world's 5.9 billion people, there are only 50 million Internet users, and over 90 per cent of Internet hosts are in North America and Western Europe. Eighty per cent of people world-wide still do not have access to a telephone (African Development Bank (ADB), 1998: 172). A quarter of countries do not yet have a teledensity of one, that is one telephone line per 100 people.

The cover of the UNDP's 1999 *Human Development Report* provides a graphic illustration of the geographic spread of the 'global enclave of Internet users' superimposed on a pie diagram showing regional distribution of global population: 'Geographic barriers may have fallen for communications, but a new barrier has emerged, an invisible barrier that is like a World Wide Web, embracing the connected and silently – almost imperceptibly – excluding the rest.'

The World Bank has spoken of its desire to 'bridge the exponentially growing digital divide between nations that are information rich and those that are not' (*World Bank Development News*, 22 February 2000). James Wolfensohn sees the Internet as an essential weapon in the battle against the huge knowledge gap. He argues that the Internet 'may be the most important determinant of what our world will look like in 50 years. Whether it be linking rural villages in India with one another, health clinics in Tanzania to hospitals in Paris, or farmers in Mali to commodity markets in Chicago, we have the power to accelerate development by generations' (*World Bank Development News*, 22 February 2000).

The International Finance Corporation (IFC), an arm of the World Bank, is to spend US$ 200 million on Internet initiatives in developing countries to jump-start the new digital economy. However, some critics argue that a focus on the basics would be more appropriate. Claire Melamed of Christian Aid cautions that 'E-commerce is not a panacea which allows developing countries to leap-frog over the need to develop basic economic and social infrastructure' (cited in *World Bank Development News*, 22 February 2000).

Significant pockets of Internet users exist in Latin America, East Asia, South East Asia and Eastern Europe and the CIS. Sub-Saharan Africa and South Asia are more poorly served. Yet even in those regions, particularly South Asia, pockets of technical expertise and access exist and a global labour market operates. Within India, the state government of Bangalore has tapped into the global market by developing software programming. For the lucky few locals who can thereby link in to the global labour market, the prospects for human security are good. However, as a strategy for broadening human security this has its limits; it is by its very nature unable to absorb labour capacity.

Mapping precarious workers

Cox's second category, precarious workers, comprises those people who may gain temporarily from the globalisation process by job creation, but who remain very vulnerable due to the pace of change in the demand for skills, and labour market conditions. In Latin America, for example, we have seen job creation accompanying growth, but 85 per cent of those new jobs are in the informal sector. Globally, the very limited numbers of new jobs created are as disappointing as is the insecurity associated with them. The pressure of global competition drives employers wherever they are located to adopt flexible labour practices, often in association with a change in national employment laws, for example, the UK, South Korea, Peru and Ukraine.

Some writers have argued that we are witnessing a feminisation of the workforce as global trade integration increases women's share of paid employment (Panos Institute, 1999: 14). This is evident in some countries, such as Bangladesh where the share of women participating in the labour force has increased from 5 per cent in 1965, to 42 per cent in 1995. The women have been employed in the garment export industry. However, that particular industry is very competitive internationally, so employment opportunities can disappear overnight. Moreover, the opportunity for such employment is a mixed blessing for the individual women concerned: in contrast to men, women's amount of unpaid workload does not diminish significantly on account of their paid work (UNDP, 1999: 81), and the conditions of employment are often undesirable.

TNCs directly employ only 3 per cent of the global labour force (Panos Institute, 1999: 6). Export processing zones provide opportunities, but employment conditions are poor. Moreover, these zones act as a magnet for migration, and this can create social problems when the expected opportunities do not materialise. In China, for example, deepening differentiation between the export-oriented coastal region of the east and the rest of the country is stark, and there is a growing problem of urban unemployment (Panos Institute, 1999: 5). The human poverty index is just under 20 per cent for the coastal regions, but more than 50 per cent in the inland province of Guizhou.

Trade liberalisation results in capital seeking out the location where it can reap the best advantage. This pits country against country, and even divides individual states – and therefore citizens – within a federal structure. An example of the latter is Brazil. When the new Governor of Rio Grande Do Sul decided to try to renegotiate contracts with Ford, other states within Brazil were quick to compete for the investment by offering more attractive loans and infrastructure to the company. The desire to attract foreign investment and the benefits expected to accompany it may result in governments diverting scarce resources away from human needs to service the needs of capital investors. It may also result in a race to the bottom, in terms of labour, environment and other social standards.

Mapping the marginalised

The outlook for Cox's third category – the expanding pool of people marginalised by the process of global economic integration – is bleak, as they are faced with increasing risk and vulnerability, and few, if any, opportunities. In the words of ILO Director General Michel Hansenne, 'The global employment situation is grim, and getting grimmer' (cited in Panos Institute, 1999: 5). Social exclusion of the most vulnerable is intensifying: the old, the young, the disabled, ethnic minority groups, the less skilled, and across all these groups there is a bias against women (ILO, 1999: 9).

Education and training can create opportunities for a limited number of people to overcome labour market exclusion, but the nature of global economic integration to date suggests that this model of development has neither the capacity nor the motivation to absorb the available labour force.

The OECD classifies 25–40 per cent of its adults as 'functionally illiterate', that is, without the necessary skills to function in the modern work environment, and thus excluded from the advantages that globalisation offers (Panos Institute, 1999: 5). If this is the situation in countries where virtually all children have the opportunity to go to primary and secondary school, the scenario for the rest of the world is very frightening indeed. World-wide, 125 million primary school-aged children never attend school. Another 150 million drop out before they can read or write (Oxfam International, 1999). Globally, this is over a quarter of the world's children. Yet there is marked differentiation across region, country and districts, and along other fault-lines such as gender. In sub-Saharan African states, 50 per cent of school-age children are not enrolled in schools. The average man in Africa has less than three years' schooling, the average women less than a year. Given that the greatest population growth takes place amongst the poor who have least access to education, without immediate remedial action we can expect differentiation to become more entrenched and to cascade into future generations. The potential for poor people to exploit learning opportunities will be affected by their malnutrition, which impairs learning ability.

The survival risks endured by marginalised people, particularly in Third World states, result not only through exclusion from the benefits of economic globalisation process, but also by the way in which that process directly undermines their ability to be self-sufficient, for example, the privatisation of the commons (Goldman, 1998). A notorious recent example of this is the redrafting of the Mexican constitution in the context of liberal restructuring in the run-up to the North American Free Trade Agreement (NAFTA). The redrafting was done to stop government redistribution of land to the landless, and to facilitate privatisation of previously communal land. While the resulting Chiapas uprising hit the global headlines, other examples can be cited from all over the world illustrating the violation of the rights of indigenous communities, landless peasants and fishing communities in order to further the interests of the holders of capital.

Polarisation in the Corporate Sector

Developing inequalities which we have seen between and within states are being replicated in the private sector, where capital is becoming more concentrated globally. A trend towards the merger of huge corporations, often occurring across territorial borders, may well exacerbate the existing problem of global monopolies.

The 1999 UNDP *Human Development Report* gives details of huge corporate mergers (UNDP, 1999: 32), including Exxon and Mobil, Chrysler and Daimler, and Hoechst and Rhône-Poulenc. Over the period 1990–97, cross-border mergers and acquisitions more than doubled, from 11,300 to 24,600. In 1997, they accounted for 59 per cent of total foreign direct investment, compared with 42 per cent in 1992 (UNDP, 1999: 31) and 58 transactions in 1997 exceeded US$ 1 billion each. The increase in total value of mergers and acquisitions has been startling in particular sectors (see Table 2.4).

Table 2.4: Total value of mergers and acquisitons, 1988 and 1998 (in US$ billion)

Sector	1988	1998
Computers	21.4	246.7
Biotechnology	9.3	172.4
Telecommunications	6.8	265.8

Source: UNDP, 1999: 67.

The trend intensified in 1998, when mergers and acquisitions totalled over US$ 2.4 trillion, over a 50 per cent increase on 1997 (see Table 2.5). Over a quarter of these deals were cross-border: 26 per cent, compared with 15 per cent in 1992 (*The Economist*, 'How to Merge After the Deal', 9 January 1999: 22). Unlike greenfield investment, mergers and acquisitons often result in job losses rather than job creation, thus fuelling the precarious nature of employment in the current era.

Table 2.5: Top ten mergers, 1998

1998	Value US$ billion
Exxon/Mobil	86.4
Travelers/Citicorp	72.6
SBC/Ameritech	72.4
Bell Atlantic/GTE	71.3
AT&T/TCI	69.9
Nations Bank/Bank America	61.6
BP/Amoco	55.0
Daimler-Benz/Chrysler	40.5
Northwest/Wells Fargo	34.4
Zeneca/Astra	31.8

Source: Securities Data Company, reprinted in *The Economist*, 2 January 1999: 5.

In the global drive for efficiency, therefore, many large as well as many small and medium-size firms are disappearing. In the case of the large firms, the majority of mergers take place within the Anglo-Saxon world. The British tend to buy American companies, and vice versa. In 1998, 80 per cent of British companies' spending on mergers and acquisitions went to the US, while 40 per cent of the US equivalent was spent on British companies. The reasons for this include similar corporate culture, and the fact that the shares of these companies are more likely to be listed and traded on the Stock Exchange than are those of other European companies (*The Economist*, 23 January 1999).

Conclusion

The global landscape of the 1980s and 1990s is characterised by increasing inequality. Whether we focus on human beings, states or corporations, this holds true. To help us understand how this situation has arisen, and the legitimacy that it has accrued, Chapter 3 considers ideas about development. In particular, we are concerned with those ideas that dominated global governance institutions – particularly international financial institutions (IFIs) – and governments over this period.

Ideas About Development

> Development can be conceived only within an ideological
> framework. (Roberts, 1984: 7)

This chapter is concerned with ideas about development,
particularly the neoliberal ideas that dominated the global
development agenda during the 1980s and 1990s and continue to
do so. The chapter begins with a brief overview of the last fifty
years, to put the discussion into a broader context. Two
approaches to development over that period are discussed: the
mainstream or orthodox approach, and an alternative approach.
This is followed by an examination of the ideas underpinning the
neoliberal development model that is generally referred to as the
Washington consensus (see below). The chapter investigates how
this consensus developed, and how it has been promoted across
the globe, especially through the activities of key global governance
institutions. Finally, the scope and depth of opposition to the
attempted universalisation of the neoliberal development model is
considered.

Development History: Orthodox and Alternative Approaches

The Orthodox Approach

Over the last half-century, a particular way of thinking about
development gained credence with international institutions like
the IMF and the World Bank, and with the majority of
governments. This approach is referred to here as the *orthodox* or
mainstream approach to development. Under this approach,
'development' referred to the change from a traditional
subsistence economy to a modern industrial economy, achieved
by an elite-driven or top-down approach reliant on the application
of modern science and technology, and 'expert knowledge' held
outside of the society to which it was to be applied. The aim was
to replicate in the South the social and economic changes that had
occurred in the North following the scientific and industrial
revolutions of the seventeenth and eighteenth centuries. Through

the application of modern science and technology on a grand scale, nature would be tamed and harnessed to serve humankind. A core idea in this approach was the possibility of *unlimited* economic growth within the context of a liberal international economy. Wealth would 'trickle down' through societies, and ultimately everyone would benefit.

While this approach remained rooted in the thinking of the Western capitalist world, some features were also shared by the conception of development held by socialist countries of the Eastern bloc. For the latter, the transformation of societies into modern industrial economies by the application of scientific knowledge and the exploitation of nature were central to the development project. The process by which this was to be achieved, however, differed. Central planning by the state, rather than reliance on the market, was the preferred method of the Eastern bloc. Ownership of property would be by the state, on behalf of the people, rather than in private hands.

The state also played an important role in the Western bloc. During the depression of the interwar period, states had pursued nationalist economic policies in an effort to export unemployment. Postwar planners such as Keynes were mindful of the contribution that they believed the economic protectionism of the 1930s had made to international instability and the outbreak of the Second World War. They were keen to construct an international economic order with a free market orientation. However, they stressed the importance of an appropriate role for state intervention in the market in order to facilitate the smooth functioning of capitalism and the promotion of global stability. Thus, a form of 'embedded liberalism' was practised, whereby states worked towards reducing barriers to trade, but recognised the political importance of state intervention in national economies. Governments were highly responsive to domestic pressures, and, for reasons of political stability and national security, were unwilling to leave everything up to the market. Full employment became a top priority. The welfare state attended to other social issues such as public health, while education and housing were also high on the agenda.

The newly independent states of the South accepted the centrality of the state sector to promote development. However, they acknowledged that they had been borne into the Western international economy and they saw their developmental opportunities and constraints within the context of that system. Many chose to follow a strategy of industrialisation through *import substitution*.

Over the period of the 1940s–1970s, Keynesian ideas dominated development theory and practice. However from the

1970s through to the present, increasingly neoclassical economic theory came to dominate. This represents a very significant ideological shift: '... whereas it was once considered normal and important for governments to intervene in at least some sectors of the economy and to provide welfare to those on the receiving ends of the cyclical crises of capitalism, we have moved to an era where such ideas are considered to be foolish at best, heretical at worst' (Wilkin, 2000). This important ideological shift is at the foundation of the global spread of the political and economic philosophy of neoliberalism, that privileges the role of the market over that of the state or other actors in determining the distribution of goods and services (see below).

International institutions such as the IMF and the World Bank promoted policies acceptable to their major funders, the Western powers, particularly the US. In the 1980s, those institutions were heavily influenced by the neoliberal ideas advocated by Presidents Reagan and Bush and the British Prime Minister Margaret Thatcher. With the demise of the communist bloc, post-1989 the IMF and World Bank universalised a particular view of development, the achievement of which was seen to depend on an enhanced role for the market and a diminished role for the state. They advocated this blueprint in regions as diverse as Eastern Europe, sub-Saharan Africa, East Asia and Latin America. This approach came to be known as the Washington consensus (see below).

An Alternative Approach

In addition to the orthodox view of development, outlined above, other critical, alternative ideas have been put forward that we can synthesise and refer to collectively as an *alternative* approach. These ideas have originated with various non-governmental organisations (NGOs), individuals, UN organisations, and private foundations. Disparate social movements not directly related to the development agenda have contributed to the flourishing of the alternative viewpoints and to the development of a more holistic approach: for example, the women's movement, the peace movement, movements for democracy and the green movements. However, it is chiefly from amongst NGOs and grassroots development organisations (GDOs) that the critical alternatives on development have arisen. (GDOs are distinguished from NGOs by being composed of the poor themselves.)

NGOs and GDOs have mushroomed in number and scope over the past two decades, but many existed before then. Many NGOs are headquartered in the South, as well as others in the North. Prominent Northern NGOs with development concerns include

Oxfam, ActionAid, the Save the Children Fund, the Catholic Fund for Overseas Development (CAFOD), World Vision and Christian Aid. Some of these Northern NGOs are more critical than others of the prevailing orthodoxy. Examples of Southern NGOs include the Malaysian-based Third World Network, the Campaign against Hunger in Brazil, the Sarvodaya Shramadana Movement in Sri Lanka, and the Freedom from Debt Coalition in the Philippines. Southern GDOs include landless peasants' movements, rural workers' unions (such as the rubber-tappers' union founded by Chico Mendes), tribal peoples' rights groups, food cooperatives, credit and savings groups, and the base ecclesiastical communities associated with the Roman Catholic Church. These groups have access to considerably fewer resources than Northern governments, multilateral development banks and Northern NGOs. Yet they continue to make important contributions to meeting the human security needs of poor people around the world. They have also played an important role in campaigning for change in the policies of the IFIs.

In contrast to the development orthodoxy, the alternative approach is very concerned about the *distribution* of the gains of the development process, as well as the appropriateness of the process itself. Table 3.1 shows in some detail the contrasting ideas of the orthodox and alternative approaches to development. Different ideas about poverty, the purpose and process of development, its core assumptions and measurement criteria are reviewed.

The Dag Hammarskjold Foundation was involved in promoting an alternative development when, in 1975, it published *What Now? Another Development* (cited in Ekins, 1992: 99). Ekins has encapsulated the alternative viewpoint: development should be:

- Need-oriented (material and non-material)
- Endogenous (coming from within a society)
- Self-reliant (in terms of human, natural and cultural resources)
- Ecologically sound
- Based on transformation of power structures (economy, society, race, patriarchy, etc.). (1992; 99)

Core elements of this essentially bottom-up alternative approach include: equitable satisfaction of basic material and non-material needs, self-sufficiency, self-reliance, diversity, appropriate (often local) knowledge, community participation, local ownership and control of policies and projects which are predominantly small-scale, and cultural, economic and environmental sustainability.

Table 3.1: The orthodox versus the alternative view of development

The Orthodox View	The Alternative View
Poverty: A situation suffered by people who do not have the money to buy food and to satisfy other basic material needs.	**Poverty**: A situation suffered by people who are unable to meet the spiritual needs of themselves and their families, and who are unable to produce enough to meet the family's material needs.
Purpose: Transformation of traditional subsistence economies defined as 'backward' into industrial, commodified economies defined as 'modern'. Production of surplus. Individuals sell their labour for money.	**Purpose**: Creation of human well-being through sustainable societies in social, cultural, political, environmental and economic terms.
Core ideas and assumptions: The possibility of unlimited growth in a broadly free market system. Economies would reach a 'take-off' point and thereafter wealth would trickle down to those at the bottom. Superiority of the 'Western' model and knowledge. Belief that the process would ultimately benefit everyone. Domination, exploitation of nature.	**Core ideas and assumptions**: Sufficiency. The inherent value of nature, cultural diversity and the community-controlled commons (water, land, air, forest). Human activity in balance with nature. Self-reliance rather than reliance on the market or external agents. Democratic inclusion, participation, e.g. voice for marginalised groups such as women, indigenous groups. Local control.
Measurement: Economic growth; Gross Domestic Product (GDP) per capita; industrialisation, including of agriculture.	**Measurement**: Fulfilment of basic material and non-material human needs of everyone; condition of the natural environment. Political empowerment of marginalised.
Process: Top-down; reliance on 'expert knowledge' usually Western and definitely external; large capital investments in large projects; advanced technology; expansion of the private sphere.	**Process**: Bottom-up; participatory; reliance on appropriate (often local) knowledge and technology; small investments in small-scale projects; protection of the commons.

Source: Thomas, 1997a: 453.

This critical approach to development remained on the periphery of global development practice and debate during the 1950–70s. However, it formed the basis for critiques that developed more forcefully over the 1980s and 1990s, in reaction to the practical experience of neoliberal development (see below, and Chapter 7).

Neoliberal Ideas: The Washington Consensus

> If I were to characterize the past decade [the 1980s], the most remarkable thing was the generation of a global consensus that market forces and economic efficiency were the best way to achieve the kind of growth which is the best antidote to poverty. (Former World Bank President Barber Conable, cited in Cavanagh et al., 1994: 3)

> ... from a small, unpopular sect with virtually no influence, neoliberalism has become the major world religion with its dogmatic doctrine, its priesthood, its law-giving institutions ... (George, 1999a)

Every society has a set of rules, which governs access to resources. Contemporary global society operates an allocation system based on neoliberal values. The neoliberal political ideology came to have a powerful influence upon the policies advocated by the world's governing elites during the 1980s and 1990s. Over that period, increasingly the market, rather than the state, determined entitlement to the fundamental material aspects of human security. This system of allocation has operated over the period when we have witnessed the deepening of inequality, as was aptly demonstrated in Chapter 2. It has exacerbated the skewed nature of access to food, shelter, education, employment, and so forth. This inequality is not perceived as a problem within the neoliberal approach; quite the opposite. Inequality is regarded as good for growth: its stimulates entrepreneurial activity, it helps generate jobs and keeps unemployment low. The growth–equity trade-off is perfectly acceptable.

John Williamson of the Institute for International Economics coined the term 'Washington consensus' to refer to the essential components of neoliberal thinking which formed the recipe for development popular in the 1980s, and especially in vogue in the 1990s. The origin of the term and its meaning are explained and summarised succinctly by Paul Krugman:

> By 'Washington' Williamson meant not only the US government, but all those institutions and networks of opinion leaders centered in the world's *de facto* capital – the IMF, World Bank, think tanks, politically sophisticated investment bankers, and worldly finance ministers, all those who meet each other in Washington and collectively define the conventional wisdom of the moment ... One may ... roughly summarize this consensus ... as ... the belief that Victorian virtue in economic policy – free markets and sound money – is the key to economic development. Liberalise trade, privatise state

enterprises, balance the budget, peg the exchange rate ...
(Krugman, 1995: 28–9)

In essence, neoliberalism argued that market forces should
determine the production, distribution and consumption of almost
all goods and services, and that the free functioning of the market
should not be distorted by government interference (see Box 3.1).
Consequently, advocates of neoliberalism favour minimum
government and *laissez-faire* economics.

Box 3.1: Free market beliefs

- Sustained *economic growth*, as measured by gross national
  product, is the path to human progress.
- *Free markets*, unrestrained by government, generally result
  in the most efficient and socially optimal allocation of
  resources.
- *Economic globalisation*, achieved by removing barriers to the
  free flow of goods and money anywhere in the world, spurs
  competition, increases economic efficiency, creates jobs,
  lowers consumer prices, increases consumer choice,
  increases economic growth, and is generally beneficial to
  almost everyone.
- *Privatisation*, which moves functions and assets from
  governments to the private sector, improves efficiency.
- The primary responsibility of government is to provide the
  infrastructure necessary to advance commerce and enforce
  the rule of law with respect to *property rights and contracts*.

Source: Korten, 1995: 70.

One of the strongest justifications for *laissez-faire* economics has
come from the philosophy of social Darwinism, which was
popularised in the writings of the nineteenth-century social
thinker, Herbert Spencer (1820–1903). It was Spencer, rather
than Charles Darwin the biologist, who coined the phrase 'the
survival of the fittest'. He believed that making welfare provisions
for the poorer members of society would retard the development
of human society as a whole, and should therefore be abandoned.
While the cruel implications of such a philosophy appear shocking,
many advocates of neoliberalism in the 1980s and 1990s came
close to adopting such a position: the welfare state should be
'rolled back' in order to eradicate the 'culture of dependency' that

it breeds, and all areas of life should be opened up to economic competition (Thomas and Reader, 1997: 9).

Neoliberalism of the 1980s and 1990s harked back to the views of the nineteenth-century 'Manchester School' liberals. However, it owes much of its recent popularity to the writings of neoclassical economic thinkers such as F. A. von Hayek (1899–1992) and his student Milton Friedman (1912–) working at the University of Chicago (see Box 3.2 for a summary of the underlying assumptions of neoclassical economics). Such writers argue that neoliberal ideas are natural and commonsensical.

**Box 3.2: Underlying assumptions
of neoclassical economics**

- Humans are motivated by self-interest, which is expressed primarily through the quest for financial gain.
- The action that yields the greatest financial return to the individual or the firm is the one most beneficial to society.
- Competitive behaviour is more rational for the individual and firm than cooperative behaviour; consequently, societies should be built around the competitive motive.
- Human progress is best measured by increases in the value of what the members of society consume, and ever higher levels of consumer spending advance the well-being of society by stimulating greater economic output.

Source: Korten, 1995: 70.

With the fall of the Berlin Wall in 1989, advocates of neoliberalism received a huge boost and felt vindicated in their grand claims. Francis Fukuyama, for example, proclaimed that the universal spread of neoliberal ideas post-1989 represents 'not just the end of the Cold War ... but the end of history as such: that is, the end point of mankind's ideological evolution and the universalisation of Western liberal democracy' (Fukuyama, 1989: 4). The collapse of the state-controlled, centrally planned economies of the former Eastern bloc symbolised 'the triumph of the West ... an unabashed victory of economic and political liberalism ... [and] the total exhaustion of viable systematic alternatives to Western [neo-] liberalism' (Fukuyama, 1989: 3).

The neoliberal approach to development stands in direct contrast to the Keynesian approach of early post-Second World War decades. During that earlier period:

The idea that the market should be allowed to make major social and political decisions; the idea that the State should voluntarily reduce its role in the economy, or that corporations should be given total freedom, that trade unions should be curbed and citizens given much less rather than more social protection – such ideas were utterly foreign to the spirit of the time. (George, 1999a)

The neoliberalism of the 1980s and 1990s therefore represents a significant departure from the embedded liberalism of the earlier period.

The Spread of Neoliberalism

The ideological and promotional work of the right has been absolutely brilliant. They have spent hundreds of millions of dollars, but the results have been worth every penny to them because they have made neoliberalism seem as if it were the natural and normal condition of humankind ... the neoliberals and their funders have created a huge international network of foundations, institutes, research centers, publications, scholars, writers and public relations hacks to develop, package and push their ideas and doctrine relentlessly. (George, 1999a)

Neoliberal ideas gained many adherents amongst professional economists in the late 1970s, and subsequently they came to have an important effect upon the policies of the New Right-influenced governments of the US and the UK. The Adam Smith Institute in the UK and the Heritage Foundation in the US played important roles in influencing government policy and sometimes advising IFIs.

In 1979, Margaret Thatcher came to power in the UK, and Ronald Reagan in the US; this heralded the beginning of a major shift to the political right in the Western world: 'Convinced that the welfare state had become so generous that it robbed individuals of discipline and initiative, believing that the growing intrusion of the state in the economy hobbled private enterprise, conservative governments aimed to roll back the state and free the market' (Rapley, 1996: 55). This shift in the Western world was to be mirrored throughout the globe.

Neoliberalism Expands through the IFIs

Since the early 1980s, the network of IFIs has been the vehicle through which the G7 industrialised states, and more particularly the US, have promoted a particular conception of development throughout the rest of the world. The IMF and the World Bank must be regarded as the principal instruments through which the doctrine of neoliberalism has obtained its current hegemony in the global order (Broad and Landi, 1996: 6; Thomas, 1998). The WTO has now taken up the mantle.

The World Bank and the IMF were profoundly affected by neoliberalism via their US-trained economic advisers and the strong role exerted by the US government in their management. The two institutions' policies are shaped by the belief of their most influential member, the US, that is, that liberalisation-driven global economic integration is the best method to promote global growth and global welfare. By exporting these ideas and the associated practices around the world, they have set the tone for the policies pursued by other multilateral development banks such as the Asian Development Bank (AsDB), the Inter-American Development Bank and the ADB.

The IFIs define the discussion of development within neoliberal parameters: economic growth through the unfettering of the market from government controls is the path ahead. They see this economic liberalisation as developing hand-in-hand with political liberalisation. For example, the Development Assistance Committee (DAC) of the OECD sees 'a vital connection ... between open, democratic and accountable political systems, individual rights and the effective and equitable operation of economic systems' (OECD, 1989).

At a structural level, the philosophy driving the policies of the IFIs in the 1980s and 1990s has supported the private sector and, by implication, a conception of civil and political rights of the individual. It has presented this as expanding human freedom through better institutions of good governance. Thus the IFIs became interested in political conditionality. It is not uncommon now for the World Bank, groups of donors and the G7 to delay or withhold funds where political liberalisation does not appear to be progressing in a manner they consider acceptable (Gillies, 1996: 101–2; Leftwich, 1994). Moreover, the EBRD has a stronger mandate in this regard.

The encouragement being given by IFIs to political liberalisation is not free of problems. Whereas the developed countries as a general rule pursued political liberalisation *after* economic development, political liberalisation is being promoted throughout the rest of the world as a *forerunner*, if not a prerequisite, of economic development. Yet the adverse consequences of economic liberalisation can undermine the consolidation of democracy. There are many instances where economic liberalisation has 'directly contributed to the descent into anarchy and civil wars' (Hoogevelt, 1997: 176), as seen in Angola, Sierra Leone, Rwanda and Sudan. Moreover, the fundamental logic of liberal democracy preceding economic development is questionable, as the authoritarian nature of the successful South East Asian tiger economies makes clear (Leftwich, 1993). It is also the case that many authoritarian governments in the Third World have not developed positive state capacity; rather they have developed the arbitrary, despotic power of the state.

The universal application of a single view of democracy is also problematic (Barya, 1993; Gills et al., 1993). The emphasis on Western-style democratic reform may give the illusion of empowering people, but without economic transformation the illusion may not be translated into anything more tangible. The interests it most effectively serves are arguably those of the holders of capital, as this type of political liberalisation creates the conditions in which foreign investment can take place more easily. Table 3.1 shows that the alternative approach to development conceptualises democracy in a different way; it calls for a more substantive democracy, based on broad participation which is only possible when access to material resources is not heavily skewed.

Under neoliberalism, the private sector is becoming more influential in affecting the fulfilment of economic and social rights (Evans, 1996, 1998, 1999; Thomas, 1998). As noted in Chapter 1, this is a cause for concern, given that the private sector's constituency is shareholders. The idea that basic needs can be met, and economic and social rights protected, in the market-place without the resources and authority of governments is dubious.

Global Conferences Lend Legitimacy to Neoliberalism

UN-organised global conferences are lending legitimacy and force to these neoliberal ideas (see Chapter 1). Moreover, these conferences are facilitating the incorporation of the language and concerns of critical alternative opinions, and thereby neutralising critical alternatives. In the 1990s, conferences constituted one of the most important institutional mechanisms to deal with development-related matters. Most noteworthy, for the broad framework they provide for understanding development, are UNCED and the World Summit on Social Development.

UNCED was important for familiarising a wider audience with the concept of 'sustainable development'. This concept had first come to public attention in the early 1980s in an International Union for the Conservation of Nature (IUCN) document (Thomas, 1992: 46). It received further emphasis in the influential *Brundtland Report* of the World Commission on Environment and Development (WCED) in 1987, which defined sustainable development as a process that 'meets the needs of the present without compromising the ability of future generations to meet their own needs' (WCED, 1987: 8). The report, also known as *Our Common Future*, highlighted the importance of maintaining the environmental resource base, and with this, the idea that there are natural limits to growth. However, the report made it clear that further growth was essential, but that it needed to be made more environment-friendly. It did not address the belief, widespread among a sector of the NGO community, that the emphasis on growth was a fundamental cause of the environmental crisis and therefore could not be the solution.

Embracing the new terminology of sustainable development, the official interstate UNCED gathering gave public acknowledgement to the idea that the environment and development are inextricably linked. It encouraged important actors such as the World Bank to assert their commitment to a 'new environmentalism, which recognizes that economic development and environmental sustainability are partners' (World Bank, 1995: ii). However, most significantly UNCED gave further legitimisation to neoliberal, market-dominated development policies. Those policies were to be the key to sustainable development.

Consequently, the conference failed to identify the global environmental crisis as part of the existing developmental paradigm. It ignored the major issues of debt, terms of trade, aid, and the consumption of resources, which formed a central part of the discussions conducted at the parallel NGO summit at Rio. Some critics have therefore concluded that, despite the apparent 'mainstreaming' of environmental concerns that occurred at UNCED, 'the old thinking about economic growth [still] prevails' and 'the old establishment that had made a living out of such economic growth has [merely] repackaged itself in green' (Chatterjee and Finger, 1994: 162). UNCED linked environment and development in name only.

The process of incorporation of alternative criticisms by the neoliberal orthodoxy continued with the 1995 UN Copenhagen Summit. The task was to address continuing and widespread poverty, inequality and unemployment. Prior to the conference, some Southern governments voiced deep dissent on issues such as debt, structural adjustment and the need to regulate TNCs. Malaysia, for example, accepted the centrality of economic growth, but argued that this was insufficient to ensure social progress. Implicitly, such countries advocated the embedded liberalism that the developed countries had enjoyed in the early postwar decades. However, the official *Summit Declaration and Programme of Action* was a testimony to the power of neoliberal advocates (Thomas, 1998). It concluded that the preferred way to tackle poverty and unemployment was the continued promotion of neoliberal free market policies and individual initiative. There were a few very watered-down references to structural adjustment, debt and the need for dialogue between the UN and the IMF/World Bank, but no mention was made of the social responsibilities of TNCs or the possibility of new transfers of finance from the North to the South. It is to the contribution of these TNCs to the spread of neoliberalism that we turn.

Transnational Corporations (TNCs)

TNCs have made a formidable contribution to the spread of neoliberal ideas. Corporations wield huge power through their vast resources – they put this power to work through lobbying, dominating the media, and through bribes for public officials, as well as spending huge sums on public relations and advertising. These activities take place not just in the developing world, but also in the developed world, ranging from specific single-issue campaigns, such as Monsanto's efforts in the UK to convince the public that there is nothing to fear from genetically modified food (Madeley, 1999: 166), to the exercise of broader influence with the motive of affecting the outcomes of the democratic process.

Their power and influence in global agenda-setting was evident at UNCED: most glaringly absent from the Rio output were guidelines – let alone regulatory policies – for TNCs. At the behest of the US, all references to TNCs were removed from Agenda 21. Yet these actors are responsible for 70 per cent of world trade, and of course their activities have important social and environmental effects. Prior to UNCED, as part of Boutros-Ghali's UN reforms, the UN Center on Transnational Corporations (UNCTC) had been dismantled. This body, under the lead of the G77 and Sweden, had been urging the formulation of internationally recognised guidelines to make TNCs more open and accountable. Thus the way was left open for these corporations to plead their own case for self-regulation. In this, they were successful. Yet there is a clear conflict between the profit motive/responsibility to shareholders, and socially and environmentally responsible corporate behaviour (see Chapters 5, 6 and 7).

Neoliberal Universalism under Fire

A broad consensus (though not unanimity – see below) has been achieved at government level on the appropriateness of the current development policies of IFIs. This reflects a consensus on the larger picture of world economic integration in which IFI activity is embedded, and on the attempted universal application of an essentially local, Western neoliberal ideology underpinning all of this. However, there is mounting evidence of dissatisfaction from other levels of global society. We can detect a variety of resistance responses in different localities to the neoliberal vision. The purpose of development is being questioned, and this questioning is intimately bound up with the rights discourse. Contemporary advocates of the critical alternative view of development believe that human insecurity will continue to be compounded rather than alleviated whilst neoliberal ideas continue to inform the mainstream approach to development.

The common thread running through the diverse examples of resistance is the rejection of the universality of the neoliberal model of development, and its portrayal instead in terms of hegemonic coercion. The model is attacked not simply for failing to deliver benefits to significant sectors of society, but for its insensitivity to cultural specificity and regional and local diversity. It is challenged for hindering, rather than facilitating, the achievement of social, economic and cultural rights for all humanity. This position is clear at the frequently cited grassroots level, but it is evident at other levels also. It is evident at the national level within domestic political arenas, and sometimes at the interstate level where there is concern about the imposition of alien values and externally driven timetables.

Resistance can take a huge variety of forms, from micro-scale to large-scale movements. When faced with such diversity, generalisation is of limited value. What follows then is simply an indicative selection organised along different levels, and reflecting experiences in different parts of the world.

Peasant Protest

In India, peasant farmers have been protesting throughout the 1990s against pro-liberalisation agricultural policies being pursued by the national and federal state governments since the 1991 World Bank/IMF adjustment package. In the South Indian federal state of Karnataka, for example, the state government, in line with trade liberalisation policies, introduced a new agricultural policy and proposals to reform the land laws to facilitate the corporatisation of agriculture in Karnataka. (For the issue of agricultural liberalisation, see Chapter 5.) This has provoked strong resistance from farmers' associations, NGOs, trade union leaders in the banking, insurance and transport sectors, environmentalists and other activists. The Karnataka farmers' union has 'been spearheading the movement against the entry of multinational corporations in agriculture' (Shiva, 1995: 33).

The Karnataka peasant farmers' protests attack the short-term policy of export agriculture promotion, which is underpinned by the removal of land-holding ceilings for aquaculture, horticulture, floriculture and agro-based industries (Shiva, 1995: 35). Vandana Shiva has highlighted five points on which these protests focus, all of which have relevance for peasants globally, and ultimately for the fulfilment of social, economic and cultural rights for all of humankind.

First, the new policy neglects the goals of sustainable agriculture and associated sustainable livelihoods by promoting unsustainable access to land, water and biodiversity. Second, it neglects food security, which is guaranteed in the Indian constitution (as well as being in the UN Covenant) by diverting the natural resources on which it depends from local communities to the requirements of exports. Third, it promotes the myth of people's participation, while privatisation, for example of water, moves control away from communities and small-scale farmers to large corporations. Fourth, the policy reverses previous gains in land reform, as evident in the recent amendment to the 1961 Karnataka Land Reforms Act. (The similar case of the reversal of land-holdings policy in Chiapas, Mexico, as a direct government response to globalisation springs to mind – see Renner, 1997: 127.) Finally, agricultural research is moved from the domain of public to private research, and therefore is driven by the profit motive rather than basic human need (Shiva, 1995: 33–5). In the process, intellectual property rights are developed to the advantage of private corporations while the rights of farmers who have husbanded seeds over generations are being neglected.

The Karnataka peasant protests are accompanied by clear alternative policies drawn up by other activist organisations; for example, the Indian Research Foundation for Science, Technology and Natural Resource Policy (RFSTNRP) has advocated 'common intellectual rights' and 'community registry' (Shiva, 1995: 35).

Resistance to economic liberalisation is also occurring at the grassroots level in the East Asian region. The process is regarded as environmentally destructive and socially iniquitous, failing to tackle redistribution issues. Grassroots organisations in East Asia are articulating sustainable development based not on private property or public ownership, but rather on the commons, on equity, environmental sensitivity, community participation in transparent decision making, and small-scale and labour-intensive projects using appropriate technology (Bello, 1997: 157–9).

Popular Resistance at the National Level

An example of national-level popular resistance to government-promoted policies supportive of neoliberal development is offered by workers' strikes in South Korea, which took place during the period December 1996–January 1997. The workers were protesting against new labour laws which had been railroaded at dawn through the National Assembly, in the absence of opposition members. The laws would delay the authorisation of multiple unions at the national level in South Korea to 2000 from 1997 as previously promised, and would directly affect job security due to clauses regarding lay-offs. The government argued that these laws were designed to help improve the competitiveness of the nation's industries at a critical economic juncture. President Kim said these laws simply upgraded existing labour legislation to the standard of advanced countries.

As support for the strike grew, white-collar workers, Buddhist monks, university professors, Catholic priests, as well as representatives of the International Confederation of Free Trade Unions, joined the industrial workers. Under mounting domestic and international pressure, the government eventually backed down.

State and Regional Resistance

In South East Asia, there is significant resistance by state-elites to the perceived US style and timetable for neoliberal development, particularly liberalisation. The South East Asian preference is for state-assisted capitalism and a subregional free trade bloc (see Chapter 7). Regional governments' actions reflect an attempt to dilute the importance of individuals and companies inherent in Western liberal economics, and to elevate the importance of communities and nations or states. Bello's account of the response of the South East Asian governments to the US push for an Asia Pacific Economic Cooperation (APEC) Free Trade Area Initiative is instructive (Bello, 1997: 151). Resisting further integration into a free market system that the US had been previously working for in its bilateral dealings with these states, they opted for a faster timetable for their own ASEAN Free Trade Area (AFTA). In addition, Malaysia has proposed the creation of the East Asia Economic group, a regional trade bloc that would exclude Australia, Canada, the US and the Latin American countries (see Chapter 7).

This resistance to the neoliberal development project in South East Asia was replicated on a wider level at the WTO Ministerial meeting in Seattle, November–December 1999, where the dissatisfaction of Third World governments with the pace, direction and process of trade liberalisation contributed to the failure of the meeting (see Chapter 7).

Global-Level Resistance

The articulation of alternative ideas occurs in the parallel NGO Forums which accompany the UN Global Summits. At the Copenhagen Summit, for example, the parallel forum severely criticised the prevailing neoliberal development model for aggravating rather than alleviating the global social crisis, and put forward its own alternative model of development based on the principles of environmental sustainability, social equity, and community participation and empowerment. The NGOs specifically identified the policies of government privatisation and trade liberalisation as being responsible for growing global inequality, and called for the immediate cancellation of debt, improved terms of trade, greater transparency and accountability of the IMF and the World Bank, and international regulation of the activities of TNCs.

The Seattle WTO Ministerial meeting was accompanied by large-scale civil society protests that played a major role in disrupting the meeting, which ended without agreement. For one analyst, the significance of the Seattle protests goes far beyond their contribution to the failure of that particular trade liberalisation meeting. Wilkin identifies the Seattle event as part of a longer history of social protest, developing especially since 1968 and gaining force with the peace movements, feminist movements, anti-racist movements and environment movements (Wilkin, 2000). For Wilkin, Seattle is very important because it 'provides a snapshot of the possibility of global solidarity and how it might be built by anti-systemic movements of apparently quite disparate interests'. The potential of Seattle then is the opportunity it offers for all those diverse, often single-issue groups, to recognise their common goal of transforming the current world order and creating something new and better by working together.

The articulation of new ideas is not confined to civil society. Whilst not forgetting current UNDP overtures to transnational capital (see Chapter 1), it is important nevertheless to mention the UNDP's efforts to legitimise a different set of development indicators. In 1990, the UNDP published its Human Development Index (HDI), and every year since it has developed and refined the ideas contained in this concept. Recognising a need to move away from conventional indicators of development based on measuring the rate of economic growth, per capita income and industrialisation, the UNDP set itself apart from the World Bank and IMF and suggested measuring life expectancy, adult literacy and local purchasing power (see UNDP, 1994). Moreover, the UNDP has also been engaged in disaggregating data for the HDI along racial, gender, regional and ethnic groups.

This has been done for the US, Brazil, China, Egypt, Malaysia, Mexico, Nigeria, South Africa and Turkey. The HDI reveals the complex and diverse nature of local situations: for example, the *Human Development Report* 1996 shows that even to disaggregate in India by gender is insufficient, for there may be disparities in female capabilities among regions, ethnic groups, or urban and rural areas (UNDP, 1996: 34).

The HDI is gaining ground as a yardstick within the UN system, but until the key global governance institutions accept it as a basis for policy, its impact on altering the fundamental parameters of the development experience of the poor will be very limited.

Conclusion

As we enter the twenty-first century, the dominant approach to development and therefore to promoting human security is more deeply rooted in neoliberal values and policies than ever before. The key to the reduction of global poverty and hunger is identified as global economic integration via free trade and the free movement of capital. This is expected to achieve the greatest possible global economic growth, which in turn is expected to result in the greatest possible contribution to global economic welfare. The key problem with this, of course, is that it does not secure an equitable distribution of the benefits of increased global economic welfare, as we saw in Chapter 2. A further problem is that it may well be environmentally unsustainable.

The expansion of the market into all areas of human life means that global resources are increasingly channelled to meet the wants of the relatively wealthy whilst the needs of the relatively poor are ignored. In other words, human security is being enhanced for a minority. The ability of the world's poor to secure their families and communities in terms of basic needs is diminishing. Neoliberal development is narrowing choice and opportunity for the vulnerable.

In response to this disempowerment, a new type of politics is evolving which is participatory and emancipatory. The range of examples is increasing daily, and this trend cannot be encapsulated neatly. The demonstrations at the WTO meeting in Seattle achieved a very high global profile. But there are many other protests which never hit the headlines, global or national. They represent a discontent with the current order, and a rich ground of alternative ideas about how best society – from the local to the global – might be organised. Our inability to formulate neat categories into which we can slot these protests should not blind us to their importance. The greatest significance of these various forms of resistance lies in the opening up of new political space in which essentially contested concepts like democracy, development, security and rights are being aired. It is clear that the neoliberal agenda is the dominant agenda, but it does not have universal legitimacy, and it is not the only agenda. State socialism may have died a death, but alternative forms of organisation and entitlement exist, others are evolving in response to need, and some are in the process of being imagined. They demonstrate that politics never stands still. The end of history has not arrived.

PART TWO

Global Development Practice in the 1980s and 1990s

CHAPTER 4

The Reform of National Economies

> ... our core mandate remains unchanged: promoting prudent
> macroeconomic management and market-oriented reforms.
> (Camdessus, 2000b).

In Chapter 3, we examined various ideas about development. This
chapter considers the role of global governance institutions,
especially the IMF and the World Bank, in translating neoliberal
ideas into development practice. The desire for structural and
institutional reform of national economies has informed the
policies of these institutions since the late 1970s. At that time,
liberal economic ideology underlay the decision by the G7 to push
a free market approach to development via structural adjustment
(Ould-Mey, 1994). It was in the 1980s and 1990s, however, that
this approach was operationalised around the globe. The chapter
begins by examining the context in which those policies arose, and
their core elements. Then different assessments of the social and
economic impact of adjustment are considered. The responses of
the IMF and the World Bank to these assessments, in terms of
policy developments, are analysed.

The Role of the IMF and the World Bank

The IMF is the linchpin in the implementation of the neoliberal
vision of development. Going beyond its original mandate to
provide short-term balance-of-payments support, it has
coordinated with the World Bank since the early 1980s to reform
national economies so that they better reflect the dominant vision
of market-led rather than state-led development. The expectation
was that this would facilitate the establishment of an environment
in borrowing countries that would attract private capital, both
domestic and foreign, and thus promote global economic
integration along free market lines. These structural and institutional reforms have redrawn the social as well as the economic
map, profoundly altering the relationship between state, market
and citizen. Regional development banks have also been drawn
into the implementation of this vision. In May 1999, for example,

the President of the African Development Bank (ADB) was asked to sign a 'memorandum of understanding' with the World Bank. Without this, the continuation of US support for the ADB was in question (EURODAD Comments, 2000).

In the 1980s, the debt crises in Latin America and Africa provided the opportunity for the IMF and the World Bank to institutionalise structural adjustment programmes (SAPs) as a debt management strategy. Post-1989, they turned their attention to the economies in transition, and more recently to East Asia. There was an unspoken agreement that adjustment and debt repayment would be rewarded by inflows of new finance and investment (see Chapter 5).

Since the beginning of the 1980s, therefore, an evolving set of conditioned structural adjustment loans has enabled the IFIs both to advance the role of the market, and to redesign the role of the state to support the creation of an enabling environment for the private sector (Mosley et al., 1991; Corner House, 1998). There has been an evolution from shorter-term SAPs to lending via the longer-term Enhanced Structural Adjustment Facility (ESAF), followed most recently by the repackaging of the ESAF as the Poverty Reduction and Growth Facility (PRGF) negotiated at the IMF in late 1999 and operational from Spring 2000.

A common core runs through these facilities. Key components of IMF and World Bank loan packages include: privatisation of public services and public assets, liberalisation of trade, finance and production, deregulation of labour and environmental laws and the destruction of state activism generally in the public realm. The market, not the state, is to be the motor of economic growth. Ultimately it will replace the state in determining entitlement of citizens to the basic necessities of human security, ranging from food, education, health care, transport and power to essential basic credit. The export-led growth expected to arise from these changes would generate the foreign exchange income necessary for countries to keep up debt repayments. (The values and assumptions underlying this development model were discussed in Chapter 3.)

The IMF and the World Bank have claimed that these policies are essentially apolitical in nature and simply reflect the 'value-free' principles uncovered by 'positive economics'. However, such a claim is questionable, since SAPs are clearly a manifestation of the neoliberal political agenda of minimal government, a *laissez-faire* free market economy, free trade, financial liberalisation and the promotion of private business interests (Thomas and Reader, 1997). The liberal belief in the acceptability of 'adjustment costs which might exacerbate inequality' (Hurrell and Woods, 1995: 452) is not universally shared. Hence the application of SAPs has resulted in social and economic impacts that are not universally considered to be acceptable. In the next section, we consider different evaluations of adjustment impacts.

Evaluating the Social and Economic Impact of Adjustment

The social and economic impact of adjustment has become a topic of heated debate. There is broad acceptance that SAPs have resulted in contradictions in ensuing patterns of entitlement. These contradictions have strained political systems and affected the fulfilment of social and economic rights that are at the heart of human security (Thomas, 1998). SAPs have had detrimental consequences for the poor and socially marginalised. In 1990, for example, *The Challenge to the South* noted that: 'The complete disregard of equity in prescriptions for structural adjustments ... had devastating effects on vital public services like health and education, with especially harmful consequences for the most vulnerable social groups' (South Commission, 1990: 67).

A consensus has emerged that there is a problem to be addressed, but opinion is bitterly divided as to the nature and extent of the problem and the appropriate path forward for achieving development for all, in particular with regard to social and economic rights. Broadly speaking, we can divide opinion into two groups: the reformers and the transformers. The former group identifies equity-related problems with the neoliberal model of development, but argues that reform is possible so as to avoid the orthodox trade-off between growth and equity. The latter group considers the neoliberal policies of the IMF and World Bank to be beyond reform and totally inappropriate in terms of meeting social and economic rights, fundamental elements of human security. Let us consider both positions.

The Reformers' Assessment

Reformers identify two central problems with ideologically driven adjustment. First, there is a gap between what works in theory and in practice. Second, domestic opposition to particular aspects, such as devaluation and the cutting of food subsidies, threatens the implementation of the reform programme (Walton and Seddon, 1994). From the late 1980s onwards, therefore, reformers, while remaining deeply committed to the broad policy of adjustment, sought changes of detail mainly to dissipate political opposition to adjustment.

The gap between theory and practice is well illustrated by the issue of credit to the poor. A feature of SAPs is the idea that such credit should be provided by the private sector, not by state or state-assisted development finance institutions such as farmers' clubs. This policy arose because of the influence of the US 'Ohio School' on World Bank policy (Hulme and Mosley, 1996: 3). Exponents of that school of development economics believed that it was impossible for any credit institutions set up by governments to avoid damage to loan portfolios via loan write-offs, and so forth. Thus the World Bank had advocated the 'closure of existing Development Finance Institutions' (Von Pischke, cited in Hulme and Mosely, 1996), hoping to create a window of opportunity for the private sector to step in.

However, the poor often do not have a point of entry into the private borrowing sector due to scarcity of investment funds and the risks of non-payment against which a lender cannot ensure, for example, the weather. The private sector naturally aims to limit its own risks. The poor therefore rely on publicly funded or backed development finance institutions:

> If ... a Malawian smallholder with two acres of maize, needing to borrow about half his average annual income for the previous five years in order to buy a 'green revolution package' of fertiliser, hybrid seed and a water pump, is unable to borrow from the state through a farmers' club, his alternative is often not to borrow it from a competitive network of informal moneylenders, but not to borrow at all. The same applies to most other poor African and Asian farmers and micro-entrepreneurs. (Hulme and Mosley, 1996: 4–5)

With the ideologically driven change in provision failing to deliver credit for the poor, reformers called for a change of policy in the 1990s. The answer of the IFIs was framed within the neoliberal approach: microfinance or microcredit (see below for details).

The most influential voice for reform was heard in 1987 when the United Nations Children's Fund (UNICEF) published the first official damning critique entitled *Adjustment with a Human Face* (Cornia et al., 1987). The report, based on ten country case studies, concluded that: 'many of the adjustment programs made no explicit effort to prevent further deterioration of the human situation in the short run – and usually relied on trickle-down from growth to improve the situation in the longer term' (Cornia et al., 1987: 288). Therefore, it argued that while adjustment to a changing world economy was necessary, there was a need for it to be designed in such a way as to ensure that the poor did not carry a disproportionate share of the adjustment burden. The UNICEF report highlighted the importance of pursuing adjustment 'with a human face'. Adjustment programmes were deflationary in character and this led to growing poverty through depressed employment and real incomes; also there were direct negative effects of certain macroeconomic policies on the welfare of particular groups (Cornia et al., 1987: 288). Therefore growth-oriented adjustment had to be devised in a manner consistent with ensuring the protection of vulnerable groups in the short and medium term. Key problems relating to adjustment to be addressed included: the short-time horizon, insufficient finance, macro as opposed to sectoral and targeted policies, and the lack of explicit consideration of the effects of programmes on income distribution, the incidence of poverty and the health/nutritional status of particular groups (Cornia et al., 1987: 288).

The report issued clear policy prescriptions for achieving adjustment with a human face (Cornia et al., 1987: 291). At the macro level these included more expansionary economic policies, aimed at sustaining output, investment and human need satisfaction over a longer adjustment period. At the meso level, prescriptions included the use of policies to prioritise and restructure resources and activities in favour of the poor. Sectoral policies were advocated, aimed at restructuring within the productive sector to strengthen employment and raise productivity, for example, focus on small farmers, improve equity and efficiency of social sectors, activate compensatory programmes, and monitor the human situation.

The UNICEF report also advocated the explicit integration of human concerns into all negotiations about adjustment, and the adaptation of the negotiation process to accommodate this. Negotiations were usually confined to the Ministry of Finance of the country concerned plus representatives of the World Bank and the IMF. Input from ministries concerned with social sectors and from international organisations concerned with nutrition was vital in the negotiation of adjustment. However, it is possible that even this recommendation did not go far enough. The illustration of privatising loans to the poor reveals that involvement of affected persons in the policy design process may yield better results. Indeed, there is growing evidence that ownership of policies, whether at local or national level, makes implementation much easier.

Since the UNICEF report, various studies of adjustment have been undertaken or funded by organisations such as the World Bank and the OECD. Several independent analyses have appeared also, such as the work of Mosley, Harrigan and Toye (1991). Killick (1994) has reviewed this reformist literature emanating from the West, and draws the following conclusions. First, he argues that generalisations are difficult, because the issues are complex and the database is totally inadequate; nevertheless, it is well documented that SAPs often put the poor at risk. SAPs are likely to impact very differently across different groups, with greater negative consequences for the urban rather than rural poor. The urban poor rely more on subsidies, government services, employment opportunities, and so forth. The poorest people are marginalised and therefore less at risk; the 'not quite so poor' stand to lose – or gain – the most. Killick believes that the negative effects of adjustment programmes have been exaggerated, and that many hardships attributed to adjustment are actually the result of pre-existing national economic crises rather than the subsequent adjustment package. Indeed, Killick's survey of available data suggests that a concentration on SAPs diverts attention away from the more fundamental causes of poverty, primarily the distribution of assets and political power. This is a point to which we shall return in Chapter 7.

The Transformers' Assessment

The basic argument of the transformers is that the overarching policy of global economic integration via free market policies, of which structural adjustment forms an important part, cannot satisfy either human security or the economic rights of states. The elevation of the private sphere, at the expense of public sphere or the commons, is a direct attack on both state sovereignty and on social, economic and cultural human rights. This transformist critique has several origins, ranging from independent authors, to UN representatives, to NGOs. A few are considered below.

Examples of independent assessments include Walden Bello's book *Dark Victory* (1994), and Michel Chossudovsky's book *The Globalization of Poverty: Impacts of IMF and World Bank Reforms* (1997). Both writers have launched trenchant critiques of the whole adjustment endeavour. Chossudovsky, for instance, has commented that:

> Structural adjustment is conducive to a form of 'economic genocide', which is carried out through the deliberate manipulation of market forces. When compared to genocide in various periods of colonial history, its impact is devastating. Structural adjustment programmmes directly affect the livelihood of more than 4 billion people. (cited by Khor, 1996: 17)

The UN Commission on Human Rights Special Rapporteur, Danilo Turk, reporting on the human rights implications of SAPs, takes a strong line. He notes that all states have legal obligations to fulfil the economic, social and cultural rights of their citizens, but the increasing integration of the world economy undermines their ability to fulfil these obligations. In particular he suggests that harm is done to the rights to work, to food, to adequate housing, to health, to education, and to development (Turk, cited by Khor, 1996: 17–18). In order to fulfil obligations to their citizens, states need first to enjoy national rights, such as the right to national ownership and to indigenous resources. These have long been a part of the struggle of developing countries for economic rights (Thomas, 1985).

Many NGOs actively pursue campaigns against structural adjustment. One of the most well-known campaigns is Jubilee 2000, which champions the cancellation of the poorest countries debt. Jubilee 2000 is strident in its rejection of SAPs, seeing them as contributing both to the unsustainable debt burden, and to the erosion of human security in recipient countries. It cannot countenance SAPs as part of the solution to the debt problem, and therefore rejects any link between debt relief and SAPs (see below).

Critics claim that the IMF and the World Bank, by organising the restructuring of the world economy along *laissez-faire* lines, and by promoting the attendant liberal conception of freedom as private power, are helping to reinforce and legitimise diverse forms of exploitation in the world economy and growing inequalities of health, income, employment opportunity, and so forth. These inequalities reflect differences in social power, and are in essence concerned with class, gender and race/ethnic relations. Transformist critics regard such growing inequalities not as contingent, but rather as the necessary outcome of social relations in a world capitalist economy.

The transformers regard the transformation of social and economic structures as essential to human security. Basic economic and social rights cannot be delivered within current structures. While acknowledging the possible pitfalls of generalisation, broadly speaking they prioritise a conception of sustainable development based around the alternative model outlined in Chapter 3.

The IMF and the World Bank Respond

How have the IFIs responded to the charges of the reformers and the transformers? It is interesting, but hardly surprising, that they ignore the transformist critique. After all, it is argued here that the IFIs represent the views of an elite that benefits from the continued liberalisation of global capital. They respond only to the concerns raised by the reformers. Therefore remarks here are confined largely to assessing how far they have taken on board the possibility of, and need for, growth with equity via reformed lending policies that protect the vulnerable.

The IMF and the World Bank are interested in limited, piecemeal reform of the existing system, rather than in the fundamental restructuring advocated by transformists. However, while these two institutions share a common world-view, they were set up for different purposes, have enjoyed different histories, have developed different policies and championed different concerns. The IMF historically has not been concerned with poverty reduction, whereas the World Bank, as a development institution, has been directly and centrally concerned with poverty. In the late 1980s and 1990s, however, both institutions became more interested in the social dimensions of adjustment, and poverty-related matters. More emphasis was put on making growth 'pro-poor'.

IMF Interest in Social Dimensions of Adjustment

It was really only in the late 1990s that the IMF began to devote real attention to poverty-reduction aspects of its programmes. Camdessus has pointed to the important role of the new Deputy Managing Director, Eduardo Aninat, former Minister of Finance of Chile. As chair of the IMF's annual meetings in the late 1990s, Aninat contributed to the debate on development, poverty and equity in income distribution. Camdessus sees Aninat's appointment as Deputy as a great strengthening of the IMF's interest and expertise in poverty-related matters.

Prior to the 1987 UNICEF report, the IMF regarded the distributional impact of its programmes as a matter for government, not IMF, concern. Indeed, a review of 30 IMF stand-by programmes implemented during the 1960s and 1970s found that only one contained provisions to protect the poor against possible adverse consequences (Bird and Killick, 1995: 33).

It appears that the UNICEF report resulted in pressure on the IMF for change, to which Fund Director Camdessus was fairly responsive. Since then it has been more accepted by the Fund that the distributional aspects of its programmes are a matter that should concern IMF staff. Policy Framework Papers prepared in connection with SAPs are required to 'identify measures that can help cushion the possible adverse effects of certain policies on vulnerable groups', and IMF missions commonly discuss distribution aspects of programmes with governments (Bird and Killick, 1995: 33–4).

Social Safety Nets

Since the late 1980s, the IMF has taken a greater interest in social safety nets. So too has the World Bank. Indeed the Bank's

Operational Guidelines were amended in 1987 to 'require analysis of the impact of adjustment programmes on the poor and attention to measures to alleviate their negative impact' (Vivian, 1995: 2–3). The Bank's concern with human capital – a healthy workforce – reinforced interest in safety nets.

Safety nets have three main aims: to alleviate the social costs of adjustment, especially poverty and unemployment; to make economic adjustment politically sustainable, and to contribute to the effectiveness of social service provisioning through social sector restructuring (Subbarao et al., 1997; Vivian, 1995). Vivian remarks that: 'These social adjustment packages ... usually involve both targeted social services and benefits, and various types of project-based social funds' (1995: 1).

The first Emergency Social Fund (ESF) was put in place in Bolivia, the prime motivation being to make structural adjustment acceptable within the Bolivian domestic political context by mitigating domestic opposition. Safety nets featured strongly in the transition countries of Eastern Europe because of their political salience: 'Attention to safety net issues is particularly important in the former socialist economies because democracy is very new, public understanding of market economics is very low, and anxiety about its social costs is very high' (Subbarao et al., 1997: 151).

In the wake of the East Asian crisis in 1997, the Fund has paid more attention to safety nets in that region. The experience in East Asia post-1997 shows that millions of people can be – indeed have been – thrown below the poverty line within an incredibly short space of time. One lesson is that financial liberalisation should not be pushed in a country until it has installed adequate regulatory institutions and proper social safety nets. Aid for the poor and unemployed should also be in place (Editorial, *Washington Post*, 7 December 1998).

The IMF, the HIPC and the PRGF

In 1996, the IMF and the World Bank initiated the Heavily Indebted Poor Countries (HIPC) initiative. This was designed to bring the debt of the poorest countries down to sustainable levels, as a reward for successful implementation of macroeconomic reform over a six-year period. Debt relief was tied to successful adherence to IMF ESAF programmes. Relief was deemed necessary in order for resources to be diverted for investment in human capital. After three years of operation, only three countries had benefited from the HIPC, and of them, one, Uganda, found itself back in an unsustainable debt position. The HIPC was heavily criticised by development NGOs such as Oxfam, and others involved in the Jubilee 2000 campaign (Watkins, 1999).

Fund interest in poverty reduction has recently been formalised in the decision to transform the ESAF into the Poverty Reduction and Growth Facility (PRGF) (Bank Information Center, 1999). This shift has been a response to political pressure, especially from the NGO community in the context of the Jubilee 2000 campaign. NGOs have criticised the IMF and the World Bank for the HIPC, which they see as being too little too late, stifling growth and undermining the building of human security. In particular, Jubilee 2000 has been vehemently critical of the link between debt relief and sustained successful implementation of ESAFs. They regard ESAFs as a cause of, rather than a cure for, poverty.

Decisions taken by the IMF Executive Board between October and December 1999 gave approval to the new PRGF, which meant the facility would become operational in early 2000. The facility is innovative in that PRGF loans will be based on a national strategy document developed with the participation of civil society. Low-income countries will receive IMF lending if their governments, in collaboration with civil society, draw up economic programmes regarded by the Fund as being in tune with stable macroeconomic policies and also bearing an element of poverty reduction. Commenting on this method, Camdessus has remarked: 'We believe that if a program is established that way and then monitored in its implementation by the public, by the civil society, the chances of sustainability, the chances of maintaining the effort long enough, will be increased' (Camdessus, 2000b).

The link with adjustment remains; however, a broader section of the population must be behind adjustment in order to see it through. The core mandate of the Fund remains unchanged, even if it may appear softer around the edges. Finding an acceptable balance between the core and the edges will not always be easy. In February 2000, the IMF's representative in Brazil, Lorenzo Perez, questioned the appropriateness of the government's ten-year anti-poverty programme, fearing that it might endanger Brazil's ability to reduce its debt. He suggested that the government might consider more effective use of the considerable money that it already dedicated to social programmes. Left and right of the Brazilian political spectrum united, seeing this as 'undue meddling' in the country's affairs. As a result, Perez had to retract his statement (Associated Press, Brazil, 12 February 2000).

The World Bank Modifies SAPs

The World Bank has a history of interest in poverty reduction. In the 1980s, the neoliberal development orthodoxy shaped its attitude to poverty reduction. The strategy shifted away from dedicated poverty reduction programmes in favour of structural adjustment programmes and policy reform.

By the mid to late 1980s, criticism of World Bank policies in terms of negative effects on the achievements of social, economic and cultural rights was resulting in some changes at the Bank. Indeed, one author claims that since 1985, 'the Bank has experienced an institutional revolution that is still in process' (de Vries, 1995: 65–80). The author attributes this directly to the activities of NGOs, which have pinpointed critical issues and put pressure on the Bank to change its policies. This, argues de Vries, has resulted in more attention on the role of women in development, environmental issues, local participation in project preparation and implementation, and greater attention to the poverty–SAP linkages.

In 1987, the Bank introduced a 'Social Dimensions of Adjustment' programme (Bird and Killick, 1995: 34) to be integrated into SAPs. Ghana's SAP was the first in Africa to formally integrate a 'Programme of Actions to Mitigate the Social Costs of Adjustment', or PAMSCAD, on the joint initiative of the government, the World Bank and UNICEF. This was deemed necessary because 'fiscal rationalization, involving the removal of subsidies and cost saving and cost recovery measures, affected health and education services' (ODI, 1996: Box 1). For example, fees were introduced into the health service and parental contributions to children's education were increased, at the same time as the number of public sector workers was cut and subsidies were withdrawn on certain agricultural inputs.

Under the PAMSCAD, US$83 million were to be spent over two years on 23 projects in five areas: education, employment generation, community initiatives, basic needs of vulnerable groups and actions to help retrenched workers. A report in 1990 concluded that only eight of the 23 projects had made good progress. A more recent assessment by the Overseas Development Institute (ODI) suggests that no real integration of social dimensions into the SAP really took place, and the measures adopted addressed pre-existing social problems rather than problems induced by the SAP (ODI, 1996: Box 1). Clearly, neither the Bank nor the government had yet met the challenge of adjustment with a human face.

A Greater Proportion of Lending for the Poor

The 1990 *World Development Report* was dedicated to poverty reduction. Since then, we have seen a growing proportion of lending devoted to poverty reduction. While in 1992, lending stood at 15 per cent, the World Bank reported that 'In fiscal year

1998, the amount lent under the programme of targeted inter-ventions increased from 29 to 40 per cent of total World Bank investment lending' (World Bank, 1999: 3). The same report also noted that in the same year 'the amount lent for poverty focused adjustment operations also increased from 52 to 64 per cent of total adjustment lending'.

Microcredit: The World Bank's Answer for the Poor

It appears that the IFIs are accepting that they have some respon-sibility for the impact of their policies on the vulnerable, even though they maintain that primary responsibility for helping such groups rests with governments. By 1996 the World Bank was clear that while 'Economic growth remains the cornerstone of the Bank's strategy for reducing poverty ... many constraints prevent the poor from benefiting from the opportunities presented by growth' (World Bank, 1996: 49). The Bank's answer is to remove such constraints, for example, by improving access of the poor, especially women, to credit.

Access to credit is an enormous problem, experienced by the poor all over the world. The creation of the Consultative Group to Assist the Poorest (CGAP) in 1995 gave a major push to the strategy of microfinance. Building on the Grameen Bank model developed in Bangladesh over two decades earlier by Professor Muhammed Yunus, the CGAP aims to reduce poverty by increasing access to small loans for very poor households through the creation of financially sustainable lending institutions. Such microfinance will enable the poor to open small businesses and thereby to earn a living – see <www.cgap.org>.

The CGAP is a multi-donor effort. The Secretariat is housed in World Bank, which is by far the largest donor. Originally involving ten partners (The World Bank, the UNDP, the ADB, the AsDB, the UN Capital Development Fund, the International Food and Agriculture Organisation, the US, the Netherlands, France and Canada), its membership has expanded to 26 with the accession of states such as Italy and organisations such as the ILO.

The CGAP pins huge hopes on microfinance, which is portrayed as the miracle that we have all been waiting for to alleviate global poverty. In the spring of 1997, the Microcredit Summit in Washington, DC, funded by, among others, Citicorp, Chase Manhattan, American Express and the World Bank, targeted 100 million people for microcredit.

In China, 85 per cent of the vast population is rural, and the lack of affordable credit is a major problem. In October 1996, the CGAP co-sponsored a microfinance conference in China with the Ford Foundation, the UNDP and local institutions. It saw this as the first chance to 'introduce international best practice in credit, savings, financial management and the formulation of financial sector policy' (Goldberg, 2000). This is directly in line with the reform of national policies, which has been the main focus of adjustment activities of the IMF and World Bank world-wide throughout the 1980s and 1990s.

All analysts do not share the faith of the World Bank and other donors in microcredit as a poverty alleviation strategy. There may be a gap between theory and practice. Weber, for example, argues that: 'in practice, microcredit may actually be reinforcing and sustaining the vicious circle of poverty at the grassroots' (Weber, 2000). Case studies suggest that if borrowers are unable to repay loans, then they will borrow from one microcredit scheme to repay another. The expected gender benefits, such as female empowerment, often do not accrue (Weber, 2000). Another critic argues that: 'While due credit must be given to Muhammed Yunus' pioneering vision, one does not have to accept the mythology created around the Grameen Bank' (Samuel, 2000: 6). For the moment, microcredit remains in vogue as a fundamental pillar in the World Bank's poverty reduction strategy. We have yet to see whether it will live up to its initial promise, but at the very least it is clear that it has a sting in its tail.

The Resilience of Neoliberal Development Ideology

Changes in detail have occurred in the positions articulated by top Bank/Fund managers regarding poverty alleviation. However, there is scant evidence that even this limited movement has yet filtered down beyond the leadership strata and resulted in real changes in operational practice. Killick argues that the Bank and the Fund 'need to go further, e.g. making it a minimum programme requirement that essential social services to vulnerable groups be maintained and in setting specific safety-net provisions into the context of a broader anti-poverty strategy' (cited in Bird and Killick, 1995: 37).

At the broadest level, the resilience of the dominant liberal economic ideology – even in the face of contrary evidence – is surprising. A good example is provided by orthodox explanations of the remarkable growth of the East Asian economies. The IMF and the World Bank emphasise that growth is dependent on further liberalisation, and that the free market is the global panacea. However, the evidence presented in the World Bank's own study, *The Asian Economic Miracle*, suggests not only that the state played a leading economic role in the development of the East Asian tigers, but that it has been the central factor in the take-off of these economies (Bello, 1997). Despite identification of the important role of state intervention, the Bank then argued this model would not be applicable elsewhere. The market held the day.

Conclusion

The IMF, the World Bank and other global governance institutions involved in the reform of national economies must regard the outcome as generally successful. The state has been displaced as the motor of development, and the market determines entitlement. The IMF and the World Bank have responded to criticisms of structural adjustment. Accordingly, their policies have evolved over the 1980s and 1990s. However, these responses have been addressed to the critiques of the reformers, and not to those of the transformers. They have been framed entirely within the context of the existing neoliberal framework, the application of which they continue to see as the solution rather than the problem. The balance between state and market has not tipped back even slightly in favour of state capacity to affect distribution and equity matters. The policies put forward to deal with the iniquitous results of growth, such as microcredit, are rooted squarely within the neoliberal orthodoxy. The continued debt repayment demanded of Mozambique by some state creditors, even in the aftermath of the floods in the spring of 2000, indicates the unwillingness of many developed countries to show flexibility even in extenuating circumstances.

CHAPTER 5

Liberalisation of Trade, Finance and Investment

In the last chapter we saw how IFIs, particularly the IMF and the World Bank, promoted the structural and institutional reform of national economies. In so doing, they created an environment conducive to the extension of the liberalisation project, which lies at the heart of the neoliberal development strategy of global economic integration. In the 1980s and 1990s, a range of actors, including not only the IFIs but also various other arms of the UN family, private banks and corporations, and business associations, promoted the liberalisation of three key areas: trade, finance and investment. Here, we focus on major policy developments during that period in each respective area, reactions to these developments, and consequent global policy responses.

Trade Liberalisation

Together, we [the IMF and the World Bank] must work with and support the work of the World Trade Organisation which is so critical to the trading arrangements and future of our client countries. (Wolfensohn, 1999a)

Trade can support livelihoods: production for export can generate income, employment, and foreign exchange which poor countries need for their development. But without adequate safeguards, trade can also destroy livelihoods, cause environmental destruction, or lead to unacceptable levels of exploitation. (LeQuesne, 1996: 1)

Trade Liberalisation at the Global Level: From GATT to WTO

This section begins with an exploration of global-level trade liberalisation, looking at the evolution of the General Agreement on Tariffs and Trade (GATT) into the WTO. Consideration is given to the expanded agenda of the WTO, and questions are asked about in whose interests this agenda is working. This is followed by an examination of regional free trade. A focus on the NAFTA experience enables us to explore how effectively trade agreements take on board the concerns of critics such as environmental and labour groups. Then we look at trade liberalisation within one sector, agriculture, to see how it affects human security. The section ends with a brief assessment of the UNCTAD.

Trade liberalisation in itself is not new. Throughout the post-Second World War period, the desire of developed countries in particular to reduce barriers to trade prompted various tariff-cutting exercises –'rounds' – via GATT. These rounds involved bargaining over tariff concessions for certain products. However, developing countries always felt that their needs were overlooked. As producers of primary commodities, they suffered from price volatility and generally declining terms of trade for their exports. Their primary concerns included the exercise of permanent sovereignty over natural resources, the right of primary commodity producers to form associations or cartels, and the index-linking of prices of primary commodities to prices of manufactured goods. They achieved little success on these issues.

From 1948 to 1997, 76 free trade agreements were created or modified, and more than half of these came into being after 1990 (ECLAC, 1997: 6). The momentum is increasing, with many more agreements planned. IMF/World Bank SAPs are in tune with the vision of the emerging world trade system as supportive of the maximal welfare of all, and of free trade as necessarily desirable. The SAPs go a long way to making national economies more amenable to free trade. Throughout the developing world and former communist countries, SAPs have contributed to the opening of previously protected domestic markets. In addition, dedicated trade liberalisation policies have been pushed at the global and regional levels. The global push is evident in the GATT Uruguay Round and in the creation of the WTO. This is reinforced and supported by the movement towards increased regional trade liberalisation, for example, the North American Free Trade Agreement (NAFTA). Transnational corporations, which account for about 70 per cent of world trade, have been forceful in their support of the trade liberalisation agenda (see Chapter 3).

Trade liberalisation became a mantra in the 1980s and 1990s. Neoliberal ideas about development stress the centrality of free trade to global economic integration. The benefits of free trade are assumed, but importantly their social implications in distributive terms do not receive attention. Possible costs of trade competition, such as impoverishment, the lowering of environmental or labour standards and other social concerns, are neglected.

The GATT Uruguay Round and the WTO

The neoliberal orthodoxy of the 1980s and 1990s lent a new vigour to the trade liberalising process. The GATT Uruguay Round extended international trade rules into two new sectors, textiles and agriculture. The Round also brought new areas previously considered as falling within domestic jurisdiction under the remit of international trade rules, and the emphasis moved from tariff to non-tariff barriers to trade (see below). The Uruguay Round culminated in the establishment in January 1995 of the WTO, which was much stronger than GATT.

Williams (1999: 153) notes that the WTO has three main elements:

- It forms the legal and institutional foundation of the world trading system;
- It provides a forum for multilateral trade negotiations, and
- It acts as a centre for the settlement of disputes between members.

Supporters have presented the organisation in a very positive light, hailing it as a technical, rule-based trade system removed from the vagaries of power. Critics, however, have posed questions relating to whose rules the WTO is upholding, and in whose interest it is working. Raghavan, for example, comments that:

> The talk of a rule-based system should not be confused with the Anglo-Saxon concept of 'Rule of Law'. It is rule-based in that in most areas covered, there are detailed rules set down on paper. By and large (except in clothing and textiles and agriculture) the rules merely carry into the international arena what the US or the EU are doing; where they had differences and could not resolve them, the rules have a great deal of ambiguity; but in some other areas, particularly involving new obligations on developing countries (such as in trade related aspects of intellectual property rights – TRIPs), the rules are specific, clear and even onerous. (Raghavan, 1997: 12)

The WTO is different from GATT in a number of ways that are discussed by Williams (1999: 155). In contrast to GATT, when states join the WTO they must accept it in its entirety. The WTO extends the GATT mandate into new areas, moving from tariff concessions and the trade in goods, to a consideration of domestic policies as they shape competition. Thus intellectual property is addressed in the WTO through the TRIPs, and likewise investment measures through the trade-related investment measures (TRIMs). The scope, permanence and rule-making authority of the WTO as compared to GATT is distinctive. The establishment of the WTO institutionalised the drive towards liberalisation, and represented a very significant step in the development of the global economic governance architecture.

The dispute settlement mechanism of the WTO is believed by supporters to offer an impartial method for resolving trade disputes. All members are bound by dispute settlement procedures. However, critics note that the interests served by these procedures are the interests of corporations, rather than the development interests of developing countries or people (Wilkin, 2000). The rules allow for cross-retaliation against parties that are unwilling or unable to follow panel recommendations, for example, the US was able to retaliate against the EU's banana regime with the Lome states by imposing tariffs on Scottish cashmere. Moreover, cross-retaliation necessarily disadvantages weak developing countries (Raghavan, 1997: 16).

Unlike many other global governance institutions, such as the World Bank and various other arms of the UN, the WTO does not have a formal consultation mechanism for NGOs (Williams, 1999: 158). However, informal consultations take place. Even without formal input, NGOs have managed to exert some influence on the WTO (see below in relation to Seattle).

The WTO agenda
The WTO agenda reflects developed countries' concerns rather than the concerns of developing countries: 'The agreement … is weighted very firmly in favour of the industrialized nations and the transnational corporations which are mostly based there' (Lequesne, 1996: 9). The expansion of the remit of the organisation into new areas, coupled with its neglect of others – such as commodities, so vital for the poorest countries – was not universally welcomed. Certain areas remain off-limits and are still subject to protectionism: 'Simply put, the core capitalist states have sought free trade agreements in areas where their companies might win out, such as financial services, intellectual property rights, and so on, whilst at the same time practicing protectionism in areas where they are potentially vulnerable to competition, such as in agriculture' (Wilkin, 2000).

In the case of the TRIPs, the identification of the WTO as the appropriate home rather than the World Intellectual Property Organization (WIPO) was seen as 'a major victory for the industrialized countries' (Neale, 1999: 119). Decisions in WIPO are taken by unweighted voting, and with developing countries representing over half the membership, outcomes in WIPO are more likely to be sensitive to developing country concerns. The push for a TRIPs at the WTO came most forcefully from the US government and from US TNCs, initially those involved in electronics and information technology, and more recently those involved with agrochemicals and biotechnology (Neale, 1999: 117).

Some developing countries, notably India, feared that the TRIPs would erode the health and food security of poorer countries that hitherto, in the absence of patents, had utilised cheap generic medicines and agrochemical products (Neale, 1999: 120). Under the TRIPs, governments must guarantee patents on new medicines. In a world where more than 50 per cent of people don't have access to essential drugs, this policy will make some important drugs more expensive rather than cheaper (Mirza, 2000: 39). The South African government, which wants to make drugs for the treatment of HIV available more widely and cheaply, is in dispute with drugs companies which are keen to protect their intellectual property rights. There is a sense in which the TRIPs seem highly protectionist: they are protecting Western pharmaceutical companies.

In the case of the TRIMs, concern has been expressed that the agreement offers benefits to TNCs while potentially damaging national development efforts. For example, the TRIMs prevent governments from requiring foreign companies to meet minimum requirements in terms of using local materials in their production processes.

Concern has been expressed that the Uruguay Round amounted to the further opening of Southern economies to TNCs, and financial and insurance industries based mainly in the North. Many in the South feared this represented an increase in the power of the already powerful, and a further weakening of those already disadvantaged. The financial benefit of the Round is not expected to reach the poorest. An OECD/World Bank report in 1994 (cited in Madeley, 1999) estimated that US$ 190 billion of the projected US$ 213 billion a year that would be added to global income by 2002 as a result of the Uruguay Round would come from reductions in tariffs and subsidies on agricultural products. The extra income would go to the traders rather than the growers, and sub-Saharan African countries would be US$ 3 billion a year worse off (Madeley, 1999: 38).

Having reviewed key aspects of trade liberalisation at the global level during the 1980s and 1990s, we turn now to the regional level, with a focus on the NAFTA experience.

Regional-Level Trade Liberalisation: NAFTA

In addition to the global-level trade liberalisation arrangements of GATT and the WTO, regional-trade liberalisation arrangements are being pursued in several areas, for example the EU, NAFTA, Asia Pacific Economic Cooperation (APEC) and the Southern

African Development Community (SADC). These are seen as supportive of global integration. In a few cases they have attempted to bring new areas into the regional trade agreements. In NAFTA, for example, environment and labour issues have been integrated into what is essentially a trade agreement through the drawing-up of side agreements. Through these side agreements, the free traders hope to accommodate the concerns of respective social movements and to ensure that the trade liberalisation project is not impeded.

NAFTA is interesting and instructive, as it represents the most significant attempt to integrate environmental concerns into a free trade agreement (Thomas and Weber, 1999). The structural and ideological push both for NAFTA and for the attached North American Agreement on Environmental Cooperation (NAAEC), otherwise known as the Environmental Side Agreement (ESA), came from the US. However, President Salinas de Gortari of Mexico provided the catalyst for the timing of NAFTA. A Harvard-educated free marketeer, Gortari wanted to take Mexico down the free market road as far and as fast as possible. He was keen to reduce the possibility of any future Mexican government returning to the protected economic path that the country had followed for so long. Mexico had not even been a member of GATT until 1985. For its part, Canada already had a free trade agreement with the US, but was keen not to be left out of a regional trade agreement, seeing advantages for weak states in multilateralism.

Public debate about NAFTA was quite strong in the US, very weak in Mexico and fairly weak in Canada (Grinspun and Cameron, 1993; Hogenboom, 1996, 1999). US environmental and labour groups campaigned hard against the granting of fast-track negotiating authority for NAFTA. Fast-tracking gives the executive the freedom to negotiate the total agreement and then to take it back to Congress for a vote on the whole package. While campaigners failed to stop the granting of fast-track authority, they succeeded in politicising the NAFTA debate within the US. President Bush and then President Clinton conceded that the trade agreement would attend to environment and labour issues. The campaigners in those respective constituencies feared that in the absence of dedicated palliative measures, NAFTA would result in the movement of US investment to Mexico, where labour and environmental standards were lower, and where enforcement was at best lax.

The main NAFTA agreement contains four clauses that relate to the environment, but mainly in the context of ensuring that trade is not obstructed. However, attached to NAFTA is the separate side agreement on the environment. The side agreement

obliges members to observe their respective domestic environmental laws. Significantly, it allows for a citizen submission
process, so that if an NGO believes a government is failing to
implement its own environmental laws, then the NGO can take
the matter to the NAAEC.

The key lesson of NAFTA's attempt to link trade and
environment is that while the agreement looks as if it has made a
link, there is little substance to this link. The NAAEC is a *side
agreement* to the main free trade agreement. There are no effective
enforcement powers to sanction countries that fail to implement
their own laws. There is no time-frame for upward harmonisation
of the respective environmental laws of the three member states.
The environmental agenda is very limited. It completely fails to
address the most serious aspects of the relationship between free
trade and the environment arising out of the integration of Mexico,
Canada and the US, and it ignores conservation issues. NAFTA
is essentially a trade agreement. Shrybman has commented that
'Trade regimes do not strengthen environmental protection unless
they are carefully and deliberately crafted to do so' (1992: 107).
NAFTA gives the appearance of having been so crafted, though
the reality is somewhat different.

Similar patterns and problems are evident with NAFTA's side
agreement on labour, the North American Agreement on Labour
Cooperation (NAALC). Just as the NAAEC fails to introduce
common minimum environmental standards or to legislate for
upward harmonisation, the NAALC fails to introduce common
minimum labour standards. As with the NAAEC, the NAALC is
geared towards each country enforcing its respective domestic laws.

Sectoral Trade Liberalisation: The Case of Food

Focusing on developments within a single sector can reveal the
cumulative social impact – ranging from the local to the global –
of trade liberalisation at the various levels reviewed above. Without
adequate safeguards, trade liberalisation can pose a serious threat
to human security. The relationship between the organisation of
agriculture and the enjoyment of the basic human right to food
provides an illustration. The state has been displaced by
agribusiness as the primary source of resources, ideas and
authority in this area (Friedmann and McMichael, cited in Saurin,
1997: 110), as TNCs supersede states in the production and
marketing of food. Agribusiness is instrumental in and responsible
for the development of new social relations and new food
insecurities (Saurin, 1997 and 1999). It is eroding the respon-
siveness and responsibility of the public domain. Since the early
1980s, SAPs have given a boost to the undermining already under

way of the national organisation of agriculture and food production. So too has the aggressive pursuit of unilateralist trade policies by the US, such as the invocation of free trade to legitimise prising open the Korean agricultural market, which had traditionally been protected by the government (Bello, 1997: 148). Global trade liberalisation, especially the Uruguay Round's Agreement on Agriculture, and regional free trade agreements such as NAFTA, are further undermining local food security and throwing peasant producers and their families off the land. The result is an increasingly global organisation of food provision and of access to food, with TNCs playing the major role.

The United Nations Conference on Trade and Development (UNCTAD)

This brief discussion of the evolving trade architecture requires a mention of the United Nations Conference on Trade and Development (UNCTAD). Established in 1964, its main purpose was to help developing countries with trade and development. Unlike GATT, which pushed the trade liberalisation agenda forward, UNCTAD did not have the clout to direct the trade agenda. Rather, its role was really to champion the cause of developing countries, in particular in relation to primary commodities, and to carry out research activities. UNCTAD was never truly supported by developed countries, and with the establishment of the WTO its role was reviewed. Some developed countries had been calling for its abolition. In the event, a review undertaken at the ninth UNCTAD conference in 1996 resulted in a change of mandate for the institution. In the words of Madeley (1999: 162), 'Its chief task now seems to be one of smoothing the path for TNC investment in developing countries.' Madeley identifies this new focus as having been developing for a few years.

Financial Liberalisation

The epoch-making change ... has been capital market opening. (Wolf, 1999)

The framing new reality of the late 20th century global financial system is that the private sector is the overwhelming source of capital for growth. (Camdessus, *World Bank Development News*, 14 December 1999)

... financial markets are inherently unstable, which can cause tremendous damage to society. (George Soros, speculator; cited in Chossudovsky, 1998)

We saw in the previous chapter that during the 1980s and 1990s, the IFIs, through their reform of national economies, created an enabling environment for private finance. Countries pursued financial deregulation in response to policy prescriptions coming from the G7, the IMF and the World Bank. The rationale for this policy was simple: developing countries often lack the domestic capital to sustain the pace of development that they desire, so capital inflows could be used to allow them to invest beyond the level permitted by their domestic savings. IFIs could then withdraw from lending.

So committed was the IMF to this strategy, that up until 1999 it actively sought to amend its Charter to enable it to require member countries to open their capital markets to overseas investors (Aslam, 2000). However, great instability has accompanied financial liberalisation, and is probably an inevitable product of it. The pursuit of financial liberalisation in the absence of proper domestic regulatory frameworks undoubtedly contributed to – indeed, some would argue, caused –the contagious financial crises experienced in the late 1990s. Aslam argues that the Asian and other financial crises from 1997 onwards diluted the IMF's enthusiasm for the strategy. Thereafter, mindful of the risks and side-effects of rapid liberalisation, the IMF advocated a more sequenced process of financial deregulation.

This section on the liberalisation of finance begins with an assessment of the nature of soaring private finance in the 1980s, and more particularly so in the 1990s. The volume (total and proportional) of this finance, its short-term, speculative nature and its exclusive twelve country targets are discussed. The role of the IMF and the issue of the global and national supervision of private finance are also examined. Then the dwindling levels of public finance are analysed, with special attention being paid to the issues of broken promises and the role of export credit agencies.

Private Finance Soars

Capital market expansion really took off in the 1990s, and this has had dramatic consequences for the nature of finance flows. In contrast to most of the post-Second World War era, development henceforth is to be financed largely through private sources rather than through a combination of multilateral and bilateral intergovernmental transfers, domestic taxation and governments borrowing from private external sources. With the development of capital markets, 'the role of the public sector increasingly shifts from providing finance to providing a framework for strong and sustainable private sector flows' (Camdessus, *World Bank*

Development News, 14 December 1999). This is the case in developed as well as developing countries.

Anderson, Barry and Honey (1998), in assessing these private flows, highlight several key points, three of which are discussed here. First, the volume of private flows has surged, both in simple monetary terms and as a proportion of overall finance. Having dropped sharply after the 1982 debt crisis, private flows recovered in the 1990s. By 1994 they surpassed both bilateral and multilateral flows, with over 70 per cent of resource flows to the developing countries coming from private market sources, another 22 per cent from bilateral aid, and only 6 per cent from IFIs. By 1996 they accounted for over 85 per cent of resource flows, dwarfing public flows. Private flows grew from US$ 44 billion in 1990, to US$ 256 billion in 1997.

Second, short-term portfolio flows have been the fastest growing, surging from US$ 3.2 billion to US$ 45.7 billion. These short-term flows are speculative rather than long term and productive, and as such have been concentrated in twelve countries – the 'emerging markets', in the preferred terminology of the World Bank's International Finance Corporation (IFC). The volume of private flows to these emerging market economies has increased from US$ 170 billion in the 1980s, to US$ 1,300 billion in the 1990s (Wolf, 1999).

These short-term speculative funds do little to promote human security. The overwhelming majority of Third World countries have been denied the opportunity to benefit from them, being largely unable to attract any type of private funds: 'Private capital has not been pouring into sub-Sahara Africa where a child today is still more likely to go hungry than to go to school' (Brown, 1996: 159). However, the denial of speculative short-term funds at least may be a blessing in disguise. The influx of this type of private capital contributes little to the safeguarding of economic and social rights: '... even though private capital has been pouring into Latin America, one third of the population still has no sanitation and ten million children still suffer from malnutrition' (Brown, 1996: 159). Moreover, the East Asian experience suggests that this type of capital, because of the instability associated with it, may actively erode human security. In that particular case, over 20 million people were thrown below the poverty line.

Third, there has been a huge proliferation of new financial instruments and institutions in the 1980s and 1990s. A few words on these new instruments such as hedge funds and other highly leveraged institutions are vital. An estimated 4,000 hedge funds exist. A large part of their activities takes place in offshore banking havens, and therefore escapes any attempts at regulation or at being brought to account by governments. The funds are very speculative, involving a high degree of risk; they carry very high returns for investors when things are going well, but spell disaster when things go wrong. They invest huge amounts, more than they hold in capital. In the case of the infamous Long Term Capital Management (LTCM), the fund manager had invested US$ 500 million for every million in capital (Chossudovsky, 1998). The leverage the hedge funds can exert is significant, with the potential to pose a challenge not only to individual countries, but also to the stability of the entire global financial system. Many banks are affiliated to hedge funds. The largest US bank, Bank America, declared a US$ 1.4 billion credit loss following the fall of the Wall Street hedge fund D.E. Shaw (cited in Chossudovsky, 1998).

Daily currency trading has shown a phenomenal rise, with an average annual increase of 55 per cent from the mid-1980s to the mid-1990s. It rose from US$ 200 billion a day in 1986, to over US$ 1.8 trillion a day in 1998. The significance of this is apparent when set against the US$ 4.3 trillion a year for the entire global trade in goods and services (DeFazio, 2000). Eighty-five per cent of this is made up of purely speculative bets on currencies and interest rates, and contributes nothing to production. Forty per cent of these transactions involve a round trip, that is, they are reversed in fewer than three days, while over 80 per cent round trip in under a week. Thirty-two per cent of these transactions take place in London; 18 per cent in the US; 8 per cent in Japan, and 7 per cent in Singapore (DeFazio, 2000). The sheer volume of these flows undermines the ability of governments through their central banks to defend their currency, and has the potential to cause great instability. This was witnessed in East Asia in 1997, Russia in 1998 and Brazil in 1999. Instability is not limited to the country of the currency under attack, but can be transmitted throughout the global financial system by a contagion effect. The human cost can be enormous.

The role of the IMF

The role of the IMF came under the spotlight with the Asian financial crisis. As the international institution with the key mandate for international financial stability, the institution was criticised for failing to predict the crisis, and also for its handling of the crisis. Some have even charged it with making the crisis worse by applying a blueprint developed in the 1980s in the context of the Latin American debt crisis, to East Asia in the 1990s. These crises were in fact very different, and required a different response. The Latin American crisis was a public sector crisis, while the East Asian crisis was a private sector crisis. The IMF was also criticised for its handling of the Russian crisis. As fast as it was lending money to Russia, capital flight was occurring. Corrupt officials were siphoning off public money and transferring it into private foreign bank accounts. The IMF has been charged with contributing to the moral hazard problem. Private banks can afford to behave recklessly, confident in the knowledge that the IMF will either bail them out or arrange a bail-out.

Supervision of private finance
Some international supervision of private finance has developed mainly through the work of the Basle Committee on Banking Supervision, but this has not kept pace with financial deregulation (*The Economist*, 'Global Finance: Time for a Redesign?', 30 January 1999). Before looking at its work, it is interesting to examine its membership. Sydney Key notes that the central bank governors of the Group of 10 (G10) set up the Committee in 1974, following the collapse of Bankhaus Herstatt in West Germany (Key, 1999: 61). Its membership comprises representatives of the banking supervisory authorities of the G10 countries: Belgium, Canada, France, Germany, Italy, Japan, Luxembourg, the Netherlands, Sweden, Switzerland, the UK and the US. There is no representation from the emerging economies or other developing countries.

The Basle Capital Accord of 1988 provided a minimum standard for bank health (McDonough, 1998: 3–12; *The Economist*, 'Capital Ideas: What's Cooking in Basle', 17 April 1999: 12). So far efforts to build on the accord have not resulted in concrete developments, due to disagreement about how to measure risk (*The Economist*, 1 May 1999: 115). However, in 1997 the Committee did publish the Core Principles for Effective Banking Supervision, which were developed with the supervisory authorities of 15 emerging market economies. Key notes: 'The Core Principles are designed to provide a generally accepted set of principles and practices for effective supervision of national banking systems that can be used throughout the world; they have been widely endorsed by supervisory authorities from both industrialised and emerging market economies' (1999: 70).

Supervision of non-bank private finance is meagre, existing mainly within the national domain. The January 1999 Basle Committee for Banking Supervision Report on Highly Leveraged Institutions, commissioned by the central bankers of the industrialised countries following the LTCM collapse, advised sounder risk management practices by banks and other lenders to highly leveraged institutions. It did not recommend regulation of the hedge funds (*The Economist*, 17 April 1999: 12). Indeed, the Bank of England has urged hedge funds to regulate themselves (Chossudovsky, 1998).

When LTCM collapsed in September 1998, with debts of more than US$ 3 billion, the US Federal Reserve Bank hosted a meeting of creditor banks. While it has denied putting public money into the rescue, its precise role is very sensitive and open to question.

Within countries, regulation of the banking system varies widely. On the whole, however, it is fair to say that 'less developed countries tend to have less regulated financial systems, financial practices are less transparent, moral hazard in the form of "crony capitalism" more prevalent and the problems of asymmetric information tend to be most pervasive' (Reinventing Bretton Woods Committee, 1999).

This makes less developed countries more vulnerable to the downsides of huge inflows or outflows. In an era of rapid capital liberalisation, these tendencies can have very significant negative consequences, not only for the country concerned but also for the international system. Crises can be contagious. Financial deregulation has proceeded at a rapid pace. The need for prudent regulation of the financial sector has received – and continues to receive – inadequate attention from individual countries and from the IFIs.

Public Finance Dwindles

Public overseas development assistance is at its lowest level in fifty years, and falling sharply. In 1996, official overseas development assistance (ODA) from the OECD was US$ 59 billion, the lowest figure in 23 years. By 1998, the figure stood at US$ 33 billion, 40 per cent down on 1990, and equivalent to 0.25 per cent of the GDP of First World countries (Wolfensohn, 1999b). Southern countries' post-Cold War fears of 'falling off the North's agenda' have been validated (Kegley and Wittkopf, 1993: 263). Despite talk of a peace dividend, the South has faced competition from the former Eastern bloc for a diminishing pool of intergovernmental assistance. Consequently, Southern governments have had to turn to other sources, primarily private foreign investors, banks, TNCs, hedge funds, other new private instruments and Northern and Southern NGOs.

Broken promises
The dwindling of public aid raises an important problem: the issue of trust in international relations. Trust is an essential component of interstate relations, as it is of all human relations. A key problem regarding development is that the governments of rich countries have made many promises, but they have failed to deliver on them. There is also the issue of unspoken promises.

Let us consider unspoken promises first. Critics argue that the IMF and World Bank have not kept their side of an unwritten bargain, that is, that adjustment and resulting debt repayment would result in new flows of investment and credit from the developed world to the developing countries. As we saw above, ODA is falling dramatically, and thus private finance is becoming proportionately more important.

In terms of spoken promises, the situation is no better. Not only is there a widening gap between the income and aid per capita of developed countries, but there is a failure to deliver on frequently reaffirmed commitments. Most noteworthy among these commitments is the target set in 1969 by the OECD, of 0.7 per cent of GNP of rich donor countries to be dedicated to ODA. Very few developed countries have reached this target, yet they continue to affirm their commitment to it even in the context of declining volumes of aid. In June 1997 the OECD's Development Assistance Committee (DAC) countries (with the exception of the US) reaffirmed their commitment to the target at the UN General Assembly Special Session (Development Initiatives, 1997: 9). To the countries of the developing world, such affirmations appear completely vacuous in the context of their experience of very diminished – and diminishing – aid flows.

The OECD DAC has reconfirmed a number of specific targets agreed in UN conferences and drawn them together in its 1996 report, *Shaping the 21st Century: The Contribution of Development Cooperation*. Developed countries have made a commitment to:

- A 50 per cent reduction in the proportion of people living in extreme poverty by 2015;
- Universal primary education by 2015;
- Eliminating gender disparity in primary and secondary education by 2005;
- A two-thirds reduction in the mortality rate for under-fives,
- A 75 per cent reduction in maternal mortality by 2015;
- Reproductive health services for all by 2015;
- Implementation of national strategies for sustainable development by 2000. (Development Initiatives, 1997: 8–9)

These goals are laudable. However, without dedicated effort to meet them, their mere existence undermines trust and confidence in North–South relations. Moreover, their repeated reaffirmation in an environment where aid flows are diminishing, and where the neoliberal ethos pervading international economic relations militates against aid flows, does more harm than good to North–South relations. Even within the context of the reduced aid that is given, much more effort is needed to ensure that a greater proportion goes to poverty eradication.

Tied aid and export credit agencies

Before drawing this section on finance to a close, it is important to say a few words about the tying of aid, which often amounts to a subsidy for exporters. Just over a quarter of OECD DAC aid is tied to the purchase of goods and services from the donor country. In addition, there is technical cooperation that is tied to services from the donor country. In 1997, this technical cooperation amounted to 40 per cent of bilateral ODA (Randel et al., 2000: 4). In the case of the UK, aid tied to trade with British companies stands at approximately 14 per cent of the aid budget.

Public finance is therefore directed not only at stimulating the private sector in recipient countries, but also at supporting the private sector at home. This is seen clearly in the developed countries' Export Credit Agencies (ECAs). These ECAs are particularly noteworthy because they are now the 'biggest class of public finance institutions supporting private sector projects, collectively exceeding in size the World Bank Group' (Norlen and Thenard, 2000). These agencies provide 'government-backed loans, guarantees and insurance to corporations from their home country that seek to do business overseas in developing countries and emerging markets' (Norlen and Thenard, 2000). Indeed, in the words of the World Bank, export credits are 'a highly competitive field' (*World Bank Development News*, 22 February 2000).

A recent UK House of Commons International Development Committee revealed that 25 per cent of all British export credit guarantees go to support armaments sales (Pilger, 2000), significantly helping the UK arms industry. This use of ECA guarantees became the focus for a political satire in the work of comedian Mark Thomas – see <www.channel4.com/Mark_Thomas>. After mounting public disquiet, in January 2000 UK Chancellor of the Exchequer Gordon Brown announced that the UK government was imposing an indefinite block on the export credit guarantee department underwriting unproductive expenditure (such as arms sales) to 63 of the world's poorest states.

Compared with arms sales to the poorest states, sales to the emerging market countries are far more lucrative. Within developed countries, there are competing interests at work within governments regarding such sales. Leaked UK Cabinet Office Minutes revealed a split in the UK government in December 1999 on the lifting of restrictions on arms sales to Pakistan. Defence Secretary Geoff Hoon and Trade and Industry Secretary Stephen Byers wanted an end to the freezing of 80 arms export licences that had been imposed following the military coup in Pakistan in October 1999. International Development Secretary Claire Short and Foreign Minister Robin Cook were opposed to this.

A campaign is underway to increase the transparency and accountability of these public-funded ECAs. Campaigners charge that many controversial projects in the developing world could not go ahead were it not for ECA backing. Yet ECAs have no development mandate, and do not have to adhere to environmental or social standards in their loans (see <www.eca-watch.org>).

Investment Liberalisation

We want corporations to be able to make investments overseas without being required to take a local partner, or export a given percentage of their output, to use local parts, or to meet any of a dozen other restrictions. (Carla Hills, US Trade Representative under the Bush Administration, cited in Korten, 1995: 123)

Power is passing from governments to TNCs and the poor are paying the highest price. (Madeley, 1999: xv)

In Chapter 4 we saw how the structural and institutional reform of national economies encouraged by the IFIs has helped to create an enabling environment for private investment, both domestic and, more importantly for this discussion, foreign. It is not surprising that those institutions should be interested in this, given their original purposes. Article 2 of the World Bank's constitution, for example, identifies the promotion of private foreign investment as one of its fundamental purposes. As early as 1956, the World Bank set up its affiliate, the International Finance Corporation (IFC), to invest in private sector companies rather than governments. In 1988, the Multilateral Investment Guarantee Agency (MIGA) was set up to encourage the flow of foreign direct investment (FDI) by providing guarantees of investments in private ventures in developing countries (ODI, 1996b: 2). In the 1980s and 1990s, the dominant ideology of neoliberalism permeating the IFIs led to a much greater emphasis on the role of the private sector in development. For example, the newest of these institutions, the European Bank for Reconstruction and Development (EBRD), set up in 1991, is compelled to direct over 60 per cent of its lending to the private sector.

TNCs: Growing Investor Power

TNCs have grown in significance throughout the 1980s and 1990s. Given current trends including the reduction in public finance, it is probable that in the future their activities will become even more important in determining the course of development within countries. In large part this can be attributed to the success of the G7, IMF and World Bank in promoting the development of a neoliberal global order in which the role of the state is redefined as a support for the private sector (see Chapter 3). Indeed, some analysts go so far as to suggest that, rather than assisting countries to achieve higher living standards for their poor, '[t]he main role of the IMF and the World Bank is the construction, regulation and support of a world system where multinational corporations trade and move capital without restrictions from nation states' (Laurence Harris, cited in Vallely, 1990: 185).

The rise of TNCs has been a key aspect of the latest phase of global economic integration. In the late 1960s there were only about 7,000, whereas in 1992 there were over 37,000 and they were responsible for US$ 5.8 trillion of sales – more than the value of all the world's trade exports put together (*Newsweek*, 26 June 1995: 35). Table 5.1 reveals that many TNCs have enjoyed greater annual sales than the GDP of individual countries.

Table 5.1: Top corporations' sales and countries' GDP, 1997

Country or corporation	GDP or total sales (US$ billion)
General Motors	164
Thailand	154
Norway	153
Ford Motor Company	147
Mitsui and Co	145
Saudi Arabia	140
Mitsubishi	140
Poland	136
Itochu	136
South Africa	129
Royal Dutch/Shell Group	128
Marubeni	124
Greece	123
Sumitomo	119
Exxon	117
Toyota Motor	109
Wal Mart Stores	105
Malaysia	98
Israel	98
Colombia	96
Venezuela	87
Philippines	82

Source: *Forbes* magazine, 1998, and UNDP, 1999: 32.

Developed countries have been keen to support TNCs by working towards a global agreement on investment that would enshrine corporate rights.

Developed Countries Seek a Global Investment Agreement

The push for investment liberalisation has formed an important part of the neoliberal strategy for global economic integration. In 1995, non-OECD countries received 38 per cent of FDI; in 1997, they received 42 per cent. As with the experience of private foreign finance, however, FDI has been directed at a very small number of countries. In 1995 over two-thirds of FDI reaching the developing world went to just eight countries, while over half of developing countries received little or none (Brown, 1996: 158). UNCTAD estimates suggest that within the countries receiving most FDI, the focus may be shifting. In 1999, Latin America received more FDI than Asia – the first time since 1986. The developed countries, from where most of the FDI originates, are keen to establish a framework to protect private investments and investors' rights. They argue that such a framework will encourage the further expansion of FDI, especially in the developing countries.

The investment issue was broached during the Uruguay Round of trade negotiations, but rejected at the insistence of developing countries. Accordingly, the discussion of investment during Uruguay was confined to specific trade-related investment matters, and resulted in the TRIMs.

However, the EU and countries such as the US, Canada, Australia and Japan wanted to secure the right of foreign companies to enter and establish themselves in any sector of the economy and in all member countries of the WTO, and also to enjoy national treatment. Therefore they promoted discussions of an investment agreement in a forum in which they could exercise influence more easily – the OECD.

The Multilateral Agreement on Investment (MAI)

Over the period 1995–98, the OECD worked hard at attempting to get an investment agreement – the so-called Multilateral Agreement on Investment (MAI). (See Chapter 1 for questions pertaining to the legitimacy of the OECD as the appropriate negotiating forum for an investment agreement of global proportions.) The aims of the MAI were higher liberalisation in general, and specifically investment liberalisation, investment protection and dispute settlement. The MAI would have removed all remaining national policy tools for regulating foreign investment and TNC activities. It would have guaranteed 'generally free entry and establishment for foreign investors, full national treatment for established investments and high standards of investment protection' (Brittan, cited in LeQuesne, 1996: 21).

In addition to the legitimacy question, other concerns were raised in relation to the MAI. The proposed agreement would have brought deep changes to investment rules, giving rights to TNCs without commensurate obligations. Martin Khor of Third World Network argued that the MAI would have serious effects on the ability of governments and people to exert a critical minimal control over their economies and social life. It would affect ownership patterns, the survival of local enterprises, employment opportunities and social and cultural life. It would directly impact on the achievement of social, economic and cultural rights of human beings and states (Khor, 1996: 21). In short, it would impact directly on human security, and contribute to human insecurity.

A global campaign to stop the MAI developed rapidly, incorporating environmental activists, labour unions and human rights campaigners, as well as many Third World governments who felt that their economic sovereignty was under attack. The campaign was successful, and the OECD bowed to public pressure and halted negotiations when the French government withdrew support.

Concerns About Investment Liberalisation

The success of the anti-MAI campaign highlights the lack of universal support for the neoliberal position that foreign investment is necessarily desirable as it will contribute to the global good. The case for the modification of corporate practice to take account of social values other than profit has gained strength over the 1990s. Interest has expanded beyond narrow campaigns on individual cases, to broader campaigns about the appropriate role of business in society.

NGOs and campaigns such as the Clean Clothes Campaign, Human Rights Watch in New York, the Organisation for Development and Peace in Canada, and Amnesty International have been scrutinising companies' policies and their actions. In addition, the UN is becoming more active in this field. It set up a new working group within its Commission on Human Rights in August 1999 to examine the effects of transnational business on human rights, and to assess the degree of compatibility between investment agreements and human rights (Capdevila, 1999). The group has a three-year term, running until August 2002.

The explosion of knowledge about corporate operations and perceived corporate complicity in the oppressive policies of many Third World regimes has fuelled interest in the relationship between transnational business activity and human rights. Ken Saro Wiwa's struggle and death on behalf of the Ogoni people in Nigeria highlighted possible connections between extraction of raw materials by TNCs, physical repression by security forces, environmental degradation and general human rights violations. The activities of BP in Colombia have also come under the spotlight. The use of child or prison labour for the production of goods for export to the markets of the First World states has been the subject of an NGO campaign. So too has the sale of diamonds to fund armaments for groups committing atrocities, for example, in Sierra Leone and Angola. In Sudan, the experience of the people of the Pariang area, mainly Dinka, is a cause of great concern. The Canadian government's *Harker Report* cites Leonardo Franco, UN Special Rapporteur on Sudan, who remarks that 'a swath of scorched earth/cleared earth territory' is being created around the oilfields. The report also notes that the government of Sudan has used the Heglig airstrip, in the Canadian company Talisman's concession, from which to launch attacks on villages by helicopter gunships and Antonovs, and abduction is becoming a major problem (*Harker Report*, 2000). Corporations are sullied by such involvement.

The development of information technology has played a vital role in this explosion of knowledge and activity around the issue of corporate responsibility. It has spurred the activities of groups working on various issues throughout the world, and facilitated collaboration and campaigning. Indeed, Kell and Ruggie suggest that:

> The effectiveness of NGOs has much to do with their ability to use the Internet to tap into broader social movements and gain media attention. Relying on hi-tech, low cost means of advocacy around single issues, they have demonstrated the effectiveness of centralized and flexible structures combined with non-formalized communication and decision-making. (Kell and Ruggie, 1999)

One author has suggested that the fall of communism has contributed to the increased interest in the social aspects of corporate behavior. Companies are now under global scrutiny, as they cannot hide behind the perceived shortcomings of other economic systems: 'So long as the inefficiencies of central economic planning were visible for comparison, the economic superiority of the market obscured its social defects. The death of Communism is not the end: it's the start of companies' full exposure to world gaze' (Chandler, 1999: 22).

Do anticipated benefits of FDI accrue?
There are worries that even the anticipated positive benefits of foreign investment may not bring the technology, skills or job creation that advocates assume to go with it. Regarding job creation, for example, Oxfam's Mayne and LeQuesne argue that in Africa and Latin America, foreign investment takes place in

capital intensive or extractive industries, where few jobs are created, and where poverty and inequality are exacerbated (Mayne and LeQuesne, 1999). They offer the example of rural Chile, where from 1987 to 1990, one of the most rapid increases in inequality on record coincided with a rapid expansion in the extraction of natural resource-based products.

A UNU/WIDER study of the effects of FDI on East and Central Europe and Russia suggests that 'the available sporadic data indicate its contribution to the growing income inequalities' (cited in Raghavan, 1998). In the same publication, a study of the Mexican experience also gives cause for concern. Foreign investment has played the major role in Mexico's spectacular export growth, but there are real questions as to who has benefited from this. The author, Michael Mortimore of ECLAC, comments: 'The jury is still out on whether the Mexican example can be considered one of immiserizing international competitiveness ... The concept implies that an economy gains international competitiveness but it does not serve to diminish the level of misery which exists in national society' (cited by Raghavan, 1998). Mortimore shows how investment by foreign TNCs has benefited the US TNCs, particularly those in the automobile and electronics industries, rather than Mexican national companies, which are not major participants in the most dynamic sectors of international trade. A development strategy based on such TNC investment may do little to help Mexicans on the ground achieve human security.

Concerns about TNCs as providers of national welfare

A particular feature of neoliberal economic restructuring that has benefited TNCs has been the privatisation of publicly owned enterprises in both the developed and the developing world (see Table 5.2).

Table 5.2: Infrastructure privatisations in developing countries, 1988–95 (million, in US$ and percentage)

Industry	Total revenues	Foreign investment	Foreign Investment as % of total revenues
Utilities (total)	11,130	3,994	35.9
(Power/gas/electricity)	(10,903)	(3,905)	35.9
(Water and sanitation)	(227)	(89)	39.4
Telecommunications	21,293	14,253	66.9
Transport (total)	7,518	2,178	29.0
(Airlines)	(6,106)	(1,739)	28.5
(Railroads)	(453)	(99)	21.8
(Road transportation)	(431)	(64)	14.8
(Ports and shipping)	(528)	(276)	52.3
Total	39,941	20,425	51.1

Source: UNCTAD, 1996: 25, cited in Finger and Lobina, 1999: 173.

This trend began in the UK and New Zealand, then spread to the developing countries and those in transition. TNCs have been able to enter sectors from which they were previously excluded for reasons of national security and national welfare, for example, telecommunications, energy production and distribution, and water (Finger and Lobina, 1999: 172). The fact that the provision of basic aspects of material human security is being placed in the hands of corporations raises some legitimate concerns.

Conclusion

Liberalisation of trade, investment and finance is propelling the change from state-led to market-driven development and human entitlement. Claims for national economic sovereignty, championed in the 1970s via the call for a New International Economic Order and also the Charter of Rights and Duties of States, have fallen by the wayside in the 1980s and 1990s with the elevation of the market above the state. National ownership and rights to indigenous resources, long a significant part of the struggle by the South to establish economic rights, have been rendered illegitimate in the drive to privatisation and in the push for unhindered foreign investment.

The implications for human security are significant. Whereas governments have formal responsibilities towards citizens, private actors such as TNBs and TNCs do not. With the private sector becoming more influential in affecting the fulfilment of basic economic and social needs, there is a cause for concern since its constituency is shareholders, and it is to them that the private sector is accountable. While their activities fundamentally affect life-chances, they do not have formal responsibility towards citizens in the way that governments do. They have no mechanisms such as the public policy of governments to address people's needs, even assuming they felt a responsibility and had the authority to do so. The idea that basic needs can be met, and economic and social rights associated with human security protected, in the market-place without the resources and authority of governments is questionable. The way liberalisation has proceeded to date appears incompatible with the realisation of human security.

PART THREE

Development Pathways for Human Security in the Twenty-first Century

The Reformist Pathway for the Twenty-first Century

> A new paradigm of development is progressively emerging ... A key feature of this is the progressive humanisation of basic economic concepts. It is now recognised that markets can have major failures and that growth alone is not enough and can even be destructive of the natural environment and of social and cultural goods. Only the pursuit of high-quality growth is worth the effort ... growth that has the human person at its center ... A second key feature is the convergence between respect for ethical values and the search for economic efficiency and market competition. (Michel Camdessus, Managing Director of the IMF, speaking at UNCTAD X in Bangkok, February 2000)

These words may appear very unexpected coming as they do from the Managing Director of the IMF, which is the linchpin of global fiscal management. In its role as a key global governance institution in the 1980s and 1990s concerned with 'balancing the budget', the IMF was not overly concerned with the adverse social implications of its policies (see Chapter 4).

But something new is happening. At the outset of the twenty-first century, largely in response to the global financial crises that spread from East Asia in mid-1997, to Russia in 1998, and to Brazil in 1999, the level of debate amongst concerned champions of the neoliberal project is increasing rapidly. This stands in stark contrast to the 1980s and 1990s, when the neoliberal supporters formed a more cohesive grouping, and when the overwhelming number of critiques originated from outside of the development orthodoxy. (Such external critiques of course continue to flourish, and these are discussed in Chapter 7.)

A new uneasiness is developing within the neoliberal camp, as awareness is heightened of the risks as well as the opportunities posed by global economic integration (Rubin, 1999). In response, neoliberalism is essentially being reformed from *within*. Henceforth, we shall refer to this as the *reformist* pathway. It is contrasted with the *alternative* pathway, addressed in the next chapter, which is trying to promote reform from *without*. In a way we can say that these two positions have evolved out of the orthodox and alternative views on development, discussed in Chapter 3, and are their most recent incarnations. (see Table 3.1, on the orthodox versus the alternative view of development).

Reformist views, specified in the above sense, emanate from the global governance institutions such as the G7, the World Bank, the IMF and the WTO, and various other arms of the UN family. They are also developed and supported by various academics, particularly in the US, who move easily between global governance institutions and governments and their academic obligations. While other actors such as TNCs and TNBs are also playing an influential role, the concern in this study is mainly with reform responses in the public global governance agencies.

As noted above, it is important to recognise that the reformists do not form a monolithic group. With the latest unfolding of financial crises, disagreements have arisen within the IMF and the World Bank and also between these institutions. Differences have sharpened between influential mainstream academic economists (mostly American) who move in and out of governance roles. Within the Group of 7, there have been many disagreements. For instance, in the wake of the Asian financial crisis, passionate disagreement surfaced between Japanese Finance Minister Eisuke Sakakibara, and the US government, whom he accused of dominating the IMF. In addition, important differences in perspective have emerged within individual governments. In the US, the 'Wall Street–Treasury complex' (see Bhagwati, 1998) has emerged as a term to refer to the closeness between the US Treasury Department and Wall Street investment bankers, a closeness not supported by all sectors of the US government or public. However, despite differences, reformists share fundamental values. At base, the reformist approach is informed by 'the fundamental belief that a market-based system provides the best prospect for creating jobs, spurring economic activity, and raising living standards in the US and around the world' (Rubin, 1999).

Core Values of Reformists

While discussion within the neoliberal camp *is* flourishing, it is still located firmly within the parameters of the Washington consensus. Thus its scope and focus remains constrained in terms of the core assumptions of neoliberal politics. These entrenched commitments – de-politicisation of the economic system, immunisation of the private sphere from demands in the name of the public, the efficacy of market efficiency in allocating social goods – remain unchallenged by the reform proposals which we are witnessing now. Therefore the latter are best understood as evolutionary adaptations within neoliberalism at the *tactical* level. For reformists, the end goal remains the same: global economic integration via the free market. However, this project is meeting with certain challenges. Thus reformists are committed to meeting these challenges by the modification of existing neoliberal policies, for the purpose of maintaining and further facilitating globalisation.

Therefore, the reformist response can best be interpreted with reference to the challenges at which it is directed. Two challenges are especially significant in terms of shaping the reform agenda. The first is the popular opposition to neoliberal policies given that global economic integration has not delivered on its promise of benefiting everyone through 'trickle down'. This elicits reformist responses that are well captured by rhetoric about institutional learning, such as the importance of 'listening to the voices of the poor'. The second is the challenge of technical obstacles to the smooth running of global economic integration. These include market-distorting subsidies, financial instability and even the role of IFIs as agencies interfering in the 'ideal market'.

James Wolfensohn, using a balance sheet analogy, aptly represents the types of reforms required to meet these two challenges. He suggests that the left-hand side of the sheet presents the language of finance ministers, that is, macroeconomic data such as national income accounts, balance of payments and trade statistics, while the right-hand side presents social, structural and human aspects (Wolfensohn, 1999a). He suggests that while the emphasis in the 1980s and 1990s had been on the left-hand side, as we enter the next millennium, we must consider both sides together.

However, it will be shown that a reformist consideration of both sides of the balance sheet stops well short of rethinking the fundamental commitments of the neoliberal conception of politics. Moreover, the proposed reforms do not typically advocate more representative structures for global governance. They do not advocate the creation of public enforcement agencies with which to adequately ensure the compliance of private interests with appropriate standards of practice. Nor do they demand sanctions for transgressors. Moreover, their interest in the right-hand side of the balance sheet does not extend to systematic monitoring of the social outcomes of neoliberal practice. The reformist agenda most definitely does not engage proactively with the problems of widespread poverty and inequality, for which it continues to reiterate the merits of 'trickle-down economics' which would ensue from greater integration. Political non-intervention remains the order of the day. *Redistribution* is not on their agenda, as this would entail an inherently interventionist approach to the delivery of politically defined social goods.

What reformists have realised is the need to secure broad-based support from an increasingly alert 'global public'. Without this, the policy prescriptions of neoliberalism will not enjoy the requisite degree of legitimacy for their continued application. Popular opposition could obstruct – even derail – the neoliberal project. Thus, emphasis has been placed on stressing values such as 'fairness', 'even-handedness,' or 'unbiased, rule-based' decision making in connection with the emerging norms of global governance. The reformist position is therefore broadly about tactics.

This chapter proceeds with an examination of particular reformist policy changes being mooted as the pathway for development in the twenty-first century. It is argued that despite heated debate within the reformist grouping, which is by no means monolithic, three core elements can be abstracted that taken together, amount to an identifiable whole:

- First, reformists want to expand the liberalisation agenda.
- Second, they want to introduce policy modifications to tackle challenges.
- Third, they want to broaden ownership of the liberalisation agenda by reaching out to potential opponents, states or civil society groups, and tying them in to the project.

To illustrate this pathway, trade, finance and investment are examined in turn. In each of these areas, we can identify an extension of the liberalisation agenda, policy modifications to accommodate problems and challenges, and a new degree of focus on broadening ownership of liberalisation policies to dampen opposition. In each area, the central thrust of the Washington consensus is being maintained under reformist policy changes. Continuity is the name of the game.

Reformists Push the Neoliberal Trade Agenda

Reformist solutions regarding trade are circumscribed by neoliberal fundamentals. The norms underpinning the Washington consensus are kept intact. For reformists, the market, not the state, must play the key role in organising trade – they believe that trade liberalisation has value in itself. The desirability of wider and deeper trade liberalisation is therefore taken for granted, and the liberalisation agenda is to be pushed forward as rapidly as possible. The assumption is that deeper global economic integration through free trade will fuel global growth. In turn, global growth will work in favour of maximising global welfare. The criteria for measuring the success of this trade agenda are the degree of trade openness achieved, and the amount of global growth generated. The former is assumed to impact positively on the latter. This assumption is sustained and legitimatised by recourse to levels of abstraction as explanations for the normative outcome. Here, the role of the 'invisible hand' comes to mind.

A Proposed New Trade Round

In keeping with this logic, support within the G7 now seems to be stronger for the WTO and its objectives. This is clear in that the WTO, as opposed to the OECD, because of its 'unbiased' rules for trade, is perceived as the appropriate home for an investment agreement (see Chapter 5 for details of the MAI). Claire Short, UK Secretary of State for International Development, voiced this in her keynote address to the WTO-initiated NGO symposium on the eve of the official opening of the WTO Third Ministerial Conference at Seattle. There, she argued: 'I remain convinced that a negotiated investment agreement reached in the WTO – where three quarters of the members are developing countries – could help developing countries to attract the investment they desperately need' (cited by Tandon, 2000). Claire Short's optimism may through a reformist reading be indicative of the motivating factor behind the G7's interest in a new trade round. The reformists' continuing commitment to the Washington consensus is clear in their advocacy of a new global round of trade negotiations, as well as stronger regional trade liberalisation. They want to keep up the momentum of the Uruguay Round, and build on its success in bringing even more new areas into the remit of the WTO.

The EU Commission in particular has been pushing for a new 'Millennium Round' of comprehensive trade negotiations at the WTO which would bring in new topics, such as investment and competition policy and government procurement. However, bringing competition policy under the purview of the WTO might work to favour large corporations over small, local businesses. The same would be true for investment policy. Liberalising the government procurement and contracting system would allow TNCs to gain contracts in domestic markets previously closed to them: for example, in education, public broadcasting and health (Barker and Mander, 2000: 37). This could be worth an estimated 3 trillion dollars (Pilger, 2000), which is not far short of the current annual total of trade in goods and services (see Chapter 5).

While reformists regard the WTO as operating beyond the vagaries of power and applying technical rules in an even-handed manner, critics prefer to ask whose rules are being applied, and in whose interest. Regarding investment, unless an agreement legislated for a proper balance between the responsibilities of

TNCs as well as their rights, then it would not help developing countries or global citizens. Developing countries however remain unconvinced both of the significance of their majority membership of the WTO, and of the value of a negotiated investment agreement to them.

Modifications suggested by the reformists which apparently cater to concerns such as social or environmental standards, may from a more critical perspective bring further problems to bear on the capacities of developing countries to pursue human security. In the absence of any *off-setting* measures with which to redress the competitive disadvantages that developing countries will experience from adopting the environmental or labour standards regimes, then these standards will merely serve to exacerbate their positional weakness.

Thus, in some instances, legislating for TNC responsibilities has been difficult, and even opposed by Third World states themselves (ICFTU, 1999). This is seen in the issues of environment and also core labour standards (Wilkinson, 1999). The US and other developed countries are interested in bringing environmental and labour issues into the remit of the WTO. Developing countries do not share the enthusiasm of the First World for these matters being brought within the trade remit. Within the US, the environmental and labour movements have lobbied hard to have their respective concerns integrated in trade arrangements (see Chapter 5 in relation to NAFTA). But developing countries have expressed fears that extending the remit of the WTO to cover these areas would be disadvantageous to them. They see the integration of trade and environment, and trade and labour standards, as protectionist moves by developed countries keen to ensure that any competitive edge enjoyed by developing countries because of lower standards or lax enforcement is lost (Raghavan, 2000: 29). The extension of the trade liberalisation agenda does not meet with universal approval.

Reformers Work to Broaden the Appeal of Trade Liberalisation

Mindful of the opposition to trade liberalistion, reformers understand the need to nurture support from potential opponents of the agenda by effectively explaining the benefits of their approach. In this sense, their response is largely tactical. This argument may be sustained by reference to the policies discussed below.

One obvious way of facilitating the migration of the trade agenda into new areas is to expand ownership of it. Reformists believe a key lesson of the breakdown of negotiations at Seattle was the importance of developing a broader consensus in support of further liberalisation. This had been recognised earlier, but not acted on with serious commitment.

In the May 1998 Ministerial Meeting, the WTO 'recognised the importance of enhancing public understanding of the benefits of the multilateral trading system in order to build support for it' (cited in EU, 1998). To this end, most G7 governments, the WTO and the EU have undertaken consultations or discussions with civil society groups (mostly from the G7 countries) active in the trade debate. Former Director General Ruggiero of the WTO has initiated outreach activities by the organisation. All these exchanges with civil society are designed to increase support for further trade liberalisation (and in the case of the US, to promote support for fast-track negotiating authority). The EU issued a statement on improving the transparency of WTO operations: 'Transparency should be part of a wider communication strategy to convey the benefits of an open multilateral trading system, explain the function and role of the WTO, as well as the interactions between trade policy and broader concerns in a global economy' (EU, 1998).

The objective of these reformist moves is to enhance the acceptability of neoliberal economic integration, as well as to pre-empt political resistance to the agenda based on arguments about the legitimacy of neoliberal global governance. Upon closer investigation, the purported concessions can be seen in themselves to advance the agenda to de-politicise the problem of the social distribution of goods.

Reformists Push the Neoliberal Finance Agenda

> ... in a world in which private markets are the overwhelming source of capital, the role of the IFIs must be to support rather than supplant private finance. (Summers, 2000)

For reformists, advancing the liberalisation of finance remains the central goal. Thus reformist proposals centre on methods to continue facilitating capital liberalisation, such as further reform of national economies to this end. From their perspective, most finance is private, and they regard this as entirely appropriate. This finance should, they believe, be privately regulated. Reforms therefore must be geared towards maintaining this situation. Most reforms address the purpose and nature of the IFIs. Reformers are less interested in working to constrain the rent-seeking behaviour of capital. This aspect of the reformist agenda works out mainly within the parameters of the Washington consensus. It is concerned with the adaptation and modification of rules, regulations and institutions with respect to their conduciveness to the smooth functioning of global economic integration. In order to 'keep politics out ', reforms are either technical, that is, directed at institutional adaptation, or they are focused on private regulation which pre-empts legislative constraints.

Recasting the Roles of the IMF and the World Bank: Summers versus Meltzer

The furthering of the neoliberal agenda on financial liberalisation is clear in the debates around the future role of the IMF and World Bank. These institutions are coming under scrutiny by reformists. US Treasury Secretary Lawrence Summers delivered a speech in December 1999 entitled 'The Right Kind of IMF for a Stable Global Financial System' (Summers, 1999). Since the US is the IMF's largest shareholder, contributing 17 per cent of IMF capital (that is, US$ 50 billion), then Summers's remarks are to be taken very seriously.

The context for Summers's remarks is the massive increase in private sector flows of finance, which he sees as necessitating a change in the role of the IMF. Summers wants to reduce the role of the IMF, streamline it and restrict it to 'core competencies' with a much reduced emphasis on the provision of finance. The focus of the IMF should be the promotion of financial stability within countries, stable capital flows between them, and rapid recoveries from financial disruptions. Recommendations included: restricting the IMF to emergency lending in the form of short-term, high-interest loans; encouraging countries to use private sector sources of finance; separating the remits of the IMF and the World Bank; demanding better accounting by recipients, and becoming more open to public scrutiny. The IMF's role in the poorest countries would be very limited, but nevertheless important, focused on promoting growth and poverty reduction. The institution itself would be modernised. Henceforth, the IMF must be a catalyst for market-based solutions: 'The IMF must be a last, and not first, resort – and its facilities and approaches should increasingly reflect that' (Summers, 1999). Importantly, however, it should not be a lender of last resort and should not underwrite risky loans at the taxpayers'·expense. This raft of reforms, if implemented, would significantly reduce the role and power of the IMF.

Summers's proposals were followed in March 2000 by the Meltzer Commission Report (Meltzer, 2000). The remit of this Commission, appointed by the US Congress, was to review reform of the IFIs. The Commission was split along political lines, with seven signatures and three dissenters. The dissenters issued their own more moderate proposals. The key recommendations of the Meltzer Report were:

- The IMF should restrict its lending to the provision of short-term liquidity to countries in financial difficulties.
- Loans would generally be made only to countries that have met preconditions for financial soundness.
- The World Bank should focus its efforts on low-income countries that lack access to capital markets
- Country and regional programmes in Latin America and Asia should be the primary responsibility of the areas' regional banks.
- The IMF, World Bank and regional development banks should write off all claims on the highly indebted poor countries 'that implement an effective economic development strategy'.
- The US should be prepared to increase significantly its budgetary support for the poorest countries.
- Regarding the World Bank, the recommendation was that it be renamed World Development Agency, and that its role be confined to making grants to the poorest. To this end, it should stop making loans to all states with a per capita income of $4,000 or above, and to countries with investment-grade bond ratings. Loans should come from private sources. (Wolf, 2000)

These suggestions bear some similarities to those of Summers; indeed Summers issued his proposals in anticipation of the main elements of the report. At a broad level, both are committed to financial liberalisation and the neoliberal approach to development. Both are concerned to foster the creation of an enabling environment for global capital, hence the Meltzer Commission's recommendation that loans would generally only be made to countries that met preconditions for financial soundness – in other words, freedom of entry and operations for foreign financial institutions (Fidler, 2000; Wolf, 2000). Both seek to reduce the role of the IMF in some sense, while increasing or at least maintaining its position of leverage between the developed and the developing countries.

In this context, however, Summers disagrees with Meltzer on a number of points which he believes will affect the ability of the US to influence the direction and policies of 'the majority of countries in which the international community has a compelling interest', in other words, the emerging economies (Summers, 2000). While Summers wants the role of the IFIs reformed, refined and reduced; he wants this done in a way which still allows the US to exert influence in the world: '... the notions that the IMF should serve only an elite club of nations, and that the World Bank's global activities should be radically scaled back, cannot be ones that the US or the international community would be wise to support' (Summers, 2000).

At a specific level, both Summers and Meltzer want a sharper delineation between the work of the IMF and that of the World Bank. Also, both want strong, targeted support for successful development in the poorest countries, and conditional debt relief for highly indebted countries with a track record of reform (Summers, 2000). The underlying agenda is the desire to shape national policies around the world in the interests of the liberalisation agenda.

Private Regulation of Private Finance

The development of private rather than public surveillance of private finance is on the reformist agenda. Alan Greenspan, Chairman of the US Federal Reserve Board, is an advocate. He has suggested that 'financial markets are too complex for public regulators to oversee'. He writes in the *American Banker*, October 1998, that: 'Twenty first century regulation is going increasingly to have to rely on private counterparty surveillance to achieve safety and soundness [of financial markets]' (cited in Chossudovsky, 1998). Thus monitoring of private finance would to be put in private hands: just as TNCs self-regulate, so private lenders will keep an eye on one another. Given the hardship and heartache for millions of people following the financial crises of the 1990s, it is troubling that Greenspan wishes to put in charge of future regulation those very actors whose imprudent pursuit of quick profit contributed to the outbreak of the crises.

Broadening Ownership by Expanding Representation

The financial crises of the late 1990s spawned several *ad hoc* groupings of states intent on discussing the reform of the global financial architecture. One important theme that recurred in various incarnations was that of representation. As we saw with trade, those committed to the liberalisation are keen to expand ownership of that agenda in order to ease its application. Jeffrey Sachs has suggested that what is needed is 'a dialogue of the rich and the poor together, not just a communion of the rich pretending to speak for the world' (1998: 22).

Some efforts are being made in this direction. In September 1999, at the annual meeting of the IMF, a new grouping, the G20, was agreed upon to consider the restructuring of global finance. Membership included the G7 countries, the EU, plus twelve countries, chosen for their significance for the global economy. These included China, India, Brazil and Russia. The IMF, the

World Bank and the EU were also invited to attend the first meeting of the group, held in Berlin in December 1999. The G20 membership represents 86.7 per cent of global GDP, and 65.4 per cent of global population. While the body has *no* decision-making power, it is a small step along the road to a more inclusive, representative debate (*World Bank Development News*, 15 December 1999).

Camdessus, as outgoing Managing Director of the IMF, called in February 2000 for the G7 annual summits to be replaced by a meeting every two years of 30 heads of governments who have executive directors on the boards of the IMF and World Bank, plus the UN Secretary-General (Wallerstein, 2000: 3). He remarked that this measure, albeit modest, 'would offer a way of establishing a clear and stronger link between the multinational institutions and a representative grouping of world leaders with unquestionable legitimacy' (Camdessus, 2000b).

Reformists Push the Neoliberal Investment Agenda

> I propose that you, the business leaders gathered in Davos, and we, the United Nations, initiate a global compact of shared values and principles, which will give a human face to the global market ... (UN Secretary-General Kofi Annan, Davos Forum, January 2000)

Reformists identify FDI by TNCs as central to the neoliberal development strategy. They are keen for FDI to continue unimpeded, and to expand. The choice facing them is clear. Geoffrey Chandler, Chair of Amnesty International's UK Business Group, argues that companies must choose between two scenarios:

> ... they can resist the extension of the boundaries of their responsibilities, as they have in the past, so jeopardizing their own reputations and – more dangerously – endangering the principle of the market system as a whole. Or they can demonstrate real corporate leadership which will underpin their economic contribution and raise their reputation. (Chandler, 1999: 23)

Reformers maintain that the promotion of global economic integration through free investment and trade is the best way to promote sustainable development, democratic polities and human rights defined in civil and political terms. The business of TNCs, they argue, helps foster growth, create wealth, employment and products for the global good. As far as possible, an enabling environment should be created for their successful operation. This of necessity must entail removing restraints on their activities and allowing them to be self-regulating global actors seeking out global advantage in a world which is borderless for capital, but not of course for people. We saw above in the section on trade that reformers are pushing for an agreement on investment at the WTO. As currently discussed in the WTO working group on trade and investment, this would significantly enhance the rights of investors without attaching obligations. The suggestion is that any public regulation that occurs, such as through the WTO, must work to protect corporate actors and the interests of capital.

However, reformists recognise that the globalisation project may be impeded by social challenges. Thus they are concerned about the bad press targeted at the activities of TNCs in the 1990s. They accept that it is important to address any significant tensions between corporate practice and society's values. The method advocated is private, not public, regulation. They believe the circle can be squared by companies' *voluntary actions* to develop responsible business practice. This is best achieved through *partnerships* between companies, governments, international organisations, employees and local communities.

Again, this approach may be said to be tactical, given that the fundamentals are not the focus of change; rather, attempts are made to incorporate a wider audience. At a broad level, the language of partnership employed by reformers in this regard promotes the idea that investment liberalisation is in all our best interests, as the most effective way to generate wealth. Business, governments and other partners can work together to further this. The task will be made easier if the fruits of the process are spread more widely, and if more people understand and shape the process by direct involvement in it. There is no need to regulate investors or investments; this is best left to the private parties themselves.

Partnerships

As noted above, reformists set great store on the value of partnerships. These serve a dual function: they help make business practice compatible with society's social values, and they expand ownership of the investment liberalisation agenda. A number of such partnership initiatives have achieved a high profile. At the global level, UN Secretary-General Kofi Annan's Global Compact is one example. In the national context, the UK's 'Millennium Challenge' is another (Committee of Inquiry, 1999: 11–14).

At the World Economic Summit (WES), in Davos, Switzerland, January/February 1999, the UN Secretary-General called on corporations to abide by core values – human rights, environment and labour standards (Annan, 1999) – via participation in a Global Compact (see Box 6.1). The Global Compact took forward Annan's previous calls at earlier WES meetings for the UN to form a 'creative partnership' with the private sector, on the basis that the two share mutually supportive goals, and because without such action the course of globalisation would be challenged. Annan pleaded: 'I call on you – individually through your firms, and collectively through your business associations – to embrace, support and enact a set of core values in the areas of human rights, labour standards, and environmental practices' (UN press release, 1 February 1999).

Annan's choice of human rights, labour standards and environmental practices as core values was not an arbitrary one. It was a direct response to the fact that interest group campaigns in these three areas were having an impact on trade and investment liberalisation. The MAI, for example, had been derailed at the OECD largely due to NGO campaigning. Concerned that the result might be restrictions attached to further liberalisation agreements, Annan declared: '... restrictions on trade and impediments to investment flows are not the best means to use when tackling [these legitimate concerns] ... Instead, we should find a way to achieve our proclaimed standards by other means' (UN press release, 1 February 1999).

Annan, like other reformers, did not suggest a binding international code of behaviour. Rather, *self-regulation* was the way forward for business, especially transnational business. Annan sees private regulation serving all those affected by a company, that is, the stakeholders – shareholders, employees, suppliers, customers, NGOs, business partners and the community.

In each of these areas – human rights, labour and environment – the Secretary General is asking business to comply with a wide range of existing international instruments and standards which have been developed for government compliance.

The Secretary General is calling on businesses to work with a variety of other partners to develop programmes in the three specified areas. These include NGOs, workers' organisations such as the International Confederation of Free trade Unions (ICFTU) and business associations such as the World Business Council on Sustainable Development (WBCSD), the International Chamber of Commerce (ICC), and the European Business Network for Social Cohesion (EBNSC).

Not all of these partners agree with the exclusive self-regulation of businesses. The ICFTU, for example, argues that 'Global and binding rules are necessary to protect people, not just property.' However, it believes that 'Voluntary initiatives can make a difference', and sees the Global Compact as potentially contributing by encouraging companies to engage in a dialogue with their global social partners – (see <www.icftu.org/english/tncs/glcindex.html>).

Box 6.1: The Nine Principles: UN Secretary-General Kofi Annan's Global Compact for the New Century

Human Rights: The Secretary-General asked world business leaders to:

Principle 1: Support and respect the protection of international human rights within their sphere of influence.
Principle 2: Make sure their own corporations are not complicit in human rights abuses.

Labour Standards: The Secretary-General asked world business leaders to uphold:

Principle 3: Freedom of association and the effective recognition of the right to collective bargaining.
Principle 4: The elimination of all forms of forced labour and compulsory labour.
Principle 5: The effective abolition of child labour.
Principle 6: The elimination of discrimination in respect of employment and occupation.

Environment: The Secretary-General asked world business leaders to:

Principle 7: Support a precautionary approach to environmental challenges.
Principle 8: Undertake initiatives to promote greater environmental responsibility.
Principle 9: Encourage the development and diffusion of environmentally friendly technologies.

Source: www.unglobalcompact.org/gc/unweb.nsf/content/thenine.htm

Voluntary, Private Codes of Conduct

In addition to the broad agenda of the Global Compact, reformists are developing and supporting a variety of methods to facilitate responsible corporate behaviour. An ILO study available on the Global Compact website offers a good overview of these tools as they relate to labour, for example, codes of conduct, social labelling and investor initiatives (<www.unglobalcompact.org/gc/unweb/nsf/content/ilostudy.htm>). A UNEP study accessed via the same site offers an overview of possibilities as they relate to the environment. These codes share two key features; they are *voluntary*, and they are *private* (Forcese, 1997; Ross, 1997; Panos Institute, 1999; Justice, 1999).

However, existence of these codes does *not* guarantee their application. To be effective, codes must be adhered to. However, independent assessments have revealed significant gaps between policy and practice (Committee of Inquiry, 1999: 24). Mark Thomas's investigations on Nestlé suggest that the company is failing to adhere to the WHO Code of Conduct on powdered baby milk – see <www.channel4.com/mark_thomas/nestle.10.html>. The problem of lack of adherence to codes is not confined to operations in the developing world. Forcese's study (1997) reveals that Canadian cigarette manufacturers, having been criticised for violating the code of conduct which forbade advertising close to schools, changed the code rather than their practice. This is not an isolated incident of non-compliance. A recent study of 360 US companies revealed that 71 had their own code of practice, but less than a third of these codes are monitored, and virtually none are monitored by independent third parties (Marlin, 1998: 40).

ISO Standards

The work of the International Organisation for Standardisation (ISO) is of particular interest for this discussion because, while its standards are private in origin, they acquire a degree of public legitimacy even though they usually lack any requirement for public or independent scrutiny. The ISO is a non-governmental organisation, bringing together representatives from about 130 countries – sometimes but not always governments. Its mission is 'to promote the development of standardisation and related activities in the world with a view to facilitating the international exchange of goods and services' – see <www.iso.ch/infoe/intro.htm>. The ISO defines its standards as 'documented agreements containing technical specifications or other precise criteria to be used consistently as rules, guidelines or definitions of characteristics, to ensure that materials, products, processes and services are fit for their purpose'. Companies can self-certify that they are operating according to an ISO standard.

Historically, ISO standards dealt mainly with the development of uniform standards in technical fields. However, recently, some generic standards have been developed which relate to general business practice and which can be audited by third parties. These include the 1989 ISO 9000 series dealing with quality assurance issues, the 1996 ISO 14000 Series, which provides systems for environmental management, and the 1999 SA8000, the Social Accountability standard on workers' rights (Panos Institute, 1999: 18).

Other Voluntary Guidelines

In addition to codes of conduct and ISOs, other *voluntary guidelines* exist for the behaviour of TNCs. An example is provided by the OECD's Guidelines for Multinational Enterprises, described by one author as 'a non-binding instrument, which nevertheless has moral force'. In contrast to the codes of conduct and ISOs discussed above, these guidelines are 'the property of all the OECD governments that were/are parties to the negotiations over their provisions' (TUAC, 1999). They serve as recommendations by member states of the OECD to companies operating within their territory. These Guidelines, first drawn up in 1976, are under review and it is expected that recommendations for changes will be made to the June 2000 meeting of OECD Council of Ministers (TUAC, 1999). Donald Johnston, Secretary General of the OECD, has remarked that 'The aim of the current review is not simply to update the guidelines – as important as that is – but also to find ways of raising their profile and making them more effective' (*International Trade Reporter*, 1999). In the wake of the failure of the MAI, the OECD is keen to improve its image and the revision of the guidelines may help with this (see Chapter 5). However, to be effective, the guidelines need to be respected, and this will be more likely if greater emphasis is placed on enforcement. Sanctions seem unlikely however, so even the revised guidelines will probably lack any real force.

Assessment

A key weakness of the reformist investment pathway was highlighted in April 2000, when, in an unprecedented move, UK Prime Minister Tony Blair asked the British company Premier Oil to downsize its operations in Burma. The reason given was that the human rights record of the Burmese government is one of the worst in the world. The company immediately refused, saying that it preferred the path of positive engagement and felt better able to monitor human rights in Burma by operating in the country. The British government had no sanction under law to require a change in the policy of the company. Ultimately, private regulation doesn't work in the interests of the global citizenry: its origin is private, it is non-binding, it has no mandatory, publicly constituted independent verification process, and it is without automatic punitive sanctions.

Conclusion: The Reformist Pathway – Business as Usual

World Bank figures available at the IMF/World Bank annual spring summit in April 2000, indicate that the UN target of a 50 per cent reduction in the absolute poor by 2015 will not be met (*World Bank Development News*, 14 April 2000). In an increasingly coordinated fashion, key global governance institutions, and the interests they represent, are overseeing a process of increased economic, political and social stratification. They are complicit in this outcome.

The reformist pathway for development in the twenty-first century, by continuing along the trajectory of the Washington consensus, represents business as usual. It will not make significant inroads into the distributional problems of global poverty or global inequality. Neither will it engage with the grim global unemployment situation. The sort of growth which Camdessus advocated in the quotation with which this chapter began, that is, growth with 'the human person at the center', is not occurring.

In the short term, the reformist pathway may temper opposition from within its own ranks. Over the medium to long term, its failure to address poverty, inequality and unemployment, plus other social issues, will make it increasingly more difficult to expand ownership of the reformist vision. In turn, this will impact on its ability to achieve its primary goal, that of expanding the liberalisation agenda. Ultimately, the reformist pathway carries the seeds of its own destruction.

CHAPTER 7

Towards an Alternative Pathway for the Twenty-first Century

> Communism vested property rights in a distant state and denied the people any means of holding the state accountable for its exercise of those rights. Capitalism persistently transfers property rights to giant corporations and financial institutions that are largely unaccountable even to their owners. (Korten, 1995: 312)

> The global financial crisis presents an opportunity to rethink and reshape the rules of the international economy so that they benefit people and the environment. (FOE–US/Third World Network/Institute for Policy Studies, 1998)

Increasing economic polarisation and widespread poverty lead many people to wonder in whose name the current global governance architecture is working. Few people have enjoyed the rewards of the neoliberal development policies of the 1980s and 1990s. Moreover, the instability accompanying the gains has devastated the livelihoods of millions, and the quality and sustainability of growth are open to question (Korten, 1995; Taylor and Thomas, 1999). Over this period, minor modifications to neoliberal policies, in response to reformist critiques, have done nothing to alleviate the concerns of the more critically minded and the politically concerned. What's more, their concerns are heightened in view of the shortcomings they perceive in the reformist development pathway currently evolving.

This chapter begins with an analysis of the core values of the alternative pathway. Then it analyses exemplars of changes being mooted as contributions to the alternative pathway to development in the twenty-first century. The alternative pathway, unlike the reformist, is not formalised in a systematic manner. It does not exist 'out there', as does the reformist. It cannot be grasped, measured, neatly packaged and put on the supermarket shelf as can the reformist. But that does not detract from its potential significance for the achievement of human security. The alternative pathway is in a dynamic state of evolution. The task here is to capture its essence. It can be considered as a set of norms that underpin evolving ideas about the appropriate nature, purpose and policy focus of governance, from the local to the global. It is argued that despite many differences within this very disparate grouping, three core elements can be abstracted that, taken together, amount to a loose yet identifiable whole:

- First, advocates of the alternative approach reject further expansion of the liberalisation agenda and posit instead the centrality of human security with its associated values (see Chapter 1).
- Second, they accept that the liberalisation achieved to date is not about to be overturned by a global revolution, and thus they are willing to work within the liberal framework to tackle the problems of poverty and inequality in a more serious manner than that suggested by neoliberal reformers. Therefore, they want to see significant policy changes in favour of redistribution.
- Third, they want to encourage the flourishing of the human security agenda by widening participation of states in global governance institutions, and by introducing more substantive participation – not simply representation – at the sub-state level.

To illustrate this alternative pathway, we examine some of the ideas being suggested regarding trade, finance and investment. In each of these areas, we can identify an opposition to further extension of the liberalisation agenda, deeper policy modifications and a new degree of focus on the state and substantive democracy. In each area, there is a desire to rein in the central thrust of the Washington consensus. A return to embedded liberalism is the name of the game, but a deeper and wider one than was experienced in the early post-Second World War decades, mindful, for example, of racial, ecological and gender issues, and this as a prelude to more far-reaching transformation.

Alternative Ideas

Current alternative ideas emanate from certain civil society groups in the Third and the First World states (such as Third World Network), some Third World governments (for example, that of Malaysia), and a small number of academics world-wide (such as Walden Bello and Michel Chossudovsky). Chapter 3 explored how an alternative model of development evolved in the 1960s and 1970s. Diverse movements such as those campaigning for peace, the environment and women's rights added extra dimensions. It was also seen in Chapter 3 that during the 1980s and 1990s more protest developed in response to the social impact of neoliberal development, and to the attempted universlisation of what was essentially a selective set of local, Western values. The neoliberal order has been experienced at a range of levels, and dissatisfaction with it has occurred over this range of experience. What distinguishes the alternative approach today is the way in which it embraces such a wide range of advocates, defined both spatially and socially. It incorporates movements from the grassroots level through the state and even regional levels. NGOs continue to play an influential role in the articulation of the alternative pathway, as does the general public through direct action such as that witnessed at Seattle in December 1999, or Washington in April 2000.

While reference is made hereafter to 'the alternative approach', there is no desire to suggest a cohesive grouping with a tight, unified vision. Various shared emergent properties, identified here as core values, have been abstracted from these diverse sources that form a loose alliance of politically sensitised individuals and groups. These groups are broadly united in their requirement for political action, and accompanying redistributive economic policies, to address the problems of global poverty and inequality that they regard as unacceptable.

Core Values

The core values of the alternative approach broadly reflect and build on those discussed in Chapter 3 and summarised in Table 3.1. *Satisfaction of human needs* is central, and applies equally to all human beings. Human needs are both *material* and *non-material*, and thus refer to the *quantitative* and *qualitative* aspects of human security discussed in Chapter 1. Human material needs are commensurate with material sufficiency, in terms of food, shelter and clothing. Non-material human needs refer to *human dignity*. This concept encompasses a range of values, including, for example, meaningful participation in the life of the community and the respect for cultural diversity. A premium on democratisation at the local, national and global levels is implicit. Substantive democracy is the goal: participation rather than mere representation at the local and national levels, and empowerment at the global governance level through wider representation of states.

The fulfilment of human needs depends, among other things, on properly functioning ecosystems. Thus human needs are related to the fulfilment of environmental needs, that is, the need for human-induced ecosystemic rupture to remain contained within parameters within which ecosystems can repair.

Importantly, however, the environment has *intrinsic*, not simply instrumental value.

The alternative pathway is dedicated to a system of *rights enshrined through duties and obligations*, which addresses these human needs. Thus, the *market has no value in itself*; rather, it acquires value if, and only if, its operation results in the satisfaction of human needs. This does not mean that all markets are necessarily undesirable. Thus it would be possible to imagine a different type of market economy to the current one, one with far greater capacity to meet human needs. David Korten envisages just such a market, composed primarily of 'family enterprises, small-scale co-ops, worker-owned firms, and neighbourhood and municipal corporations' (1995: 312).

Put simply, *an economic system, to be valued, must work for people and also for the planet*. Thus, the distribution of the benefits of trade, finance and investment are central to a determination of their appropriateness. The legitimacy of arrangements in each of these spheres is determined by whether the outcome is regarded as rewarding all parties sufficiently. The neoliberal criterion of the maximisation of global wealth creation is irrelevant. Rather, the specific, disaggregated effects of an economic system on the experience of income poverty and human poverty are important (see Chapter 1).

Experience of the last two decades has resulted in a distrust of the competitive, market-oriented policies aimed at growth, liberalisation and global economic integration. Instead, faith is invested in the public sphere, the state and ultimately the locality, and trust is placed in cooperation. Exponents of the alternative pathway believe that politics, not an impersonal market, must drive social policy. They believe in political intervention in the economy by the state, operating with a mandate from citizens. The government has the responsibility to implement policies to achieve redistribution, to tackle poverty and boost employment. They also believe in redistributive global mechanisms. Regulation of economic activity at the national and global levels in support of human needs is essential.

While the ultimate goal of the alternative approach is fundamental transformation of existing economic and political structures, supporters are willing in the short and medium term to focus on more limited policy changes. However, it is important to differentiate between these policy changes, and the tactical changes of reformers. The overriding goals are different. For reformers, the continuation and extension of the neoliberal project is the goal, and this is to be supported by the use of conciliatory policies to broaden ownership of the agenda. For the alternative approach, the overriding goal is redistribution in support of human needs satisfaction. In the absence of completely overturning existing global structures, this goal can be supported in the short and medium term by modifications to the existing neoliberal framework, and represents a pragmatic approach. Some improvements are better than none, so long as we do not lose sight of the ultimate goal.

Such modifications require a much greater role for the state than under the reformist approach. Thus the alternative approach supports the agenda articulated a quarter of a century ago by Third World states in the CERDS, but they go further: they want national and as far as possible, local, authorship, ownership and control over, development policies. This is a long-term perspective. The needs of individual states as determined by national governments must be given priority over the needs of capital. Liberalisation, whether of trade, finance, or investment, must take place only at the pace appropriate to the specific country concerned as determined by the government, with a mandate from citizens.

Pursuing the Vision: Short-term Modification, Long-term Transformation

Having considered the values that inform the purpose of the alternative pathway, it will be helpful to consider how over time the approach could result in a more systematic framework. Thus, we now turn to an exploration of attempts to strengthen the human security imperative within the existing development framework, as a step on the road to deeper transformation over the long term. We consider an indicative selection of policies drawn from the areas of trade, finance and investment, paying most attention to the global level, for that is the focus of this study. However, the significance of the state level, which is crucial to the alternative pathway, is also highlighted.

Investment: Regulation is the Path Ahead

Corporations are only a means of meeting human needs. (Korten, 1995: 324).

The alternative approach sees the purpose of investment as not simply – or even primarily – to generate profit for shareholders, but rather to help the community in which the investment takes place by contributing to locally and nationally determined sustainable development strategies. Susan George argues: 'Business and the market have their place, but this place cannot occupy the entire sphere of human existence' (George, 1999a).

Investments must go further than simply showing sensitivity to broader goals than profit: they must positively facilitate the promotion of human rights defined not in the narrow civil and political sense but in the broader sense, which includes economic and social rights as well. Self-regulation of corporations via voluntary codes of conduct are wholly inadequate and open to abuse, not only within the Third World but also within the First. Hence, *public regulation of corporations is essential,* and this can occur at the national and global levels. The primary purpose of regulation must be the protection of countries and local communities, not private property. The Citizen's Agenda for the Reform of the Global Economic System, drawn up and signed by dozens of NGOs world-wide, argues that governments must:

- have the right to regulate investment,
- establish measures to redirect and improve the quality of FDI flows,
- review and renegotiate international institutions and agreements concerning investments,
- participate in the establishment of core standards of behaviour for TNCs and their effective monitoring and enforcement, and
- re-examine corporate structure and activities. (FOE-US/TWN/IPS, 1998)

These views recall and develop the concerns for economic sovereignty, particularly permanent sovereignty over natural resources expressed two-and-a-half decades previously in the NIEO and CERDS.

A mandatory global code of conduct
The establishment of a *mandatory global code of conduct* would go a long way to helping make corporations publicly accountable. Supporters of the alternative approach recall moves by the Third World states in the 1970s to establish such a code. At that time, the involvement of a US company, AT&T, in the *coup d'état* in Chile contributed to the setting-up of the UNCTC. The efforts of the UNCTC to establish such a code lost momentum in the 1980s with the rise of neoliberalism. In the 1990s enthusiasm grew for protecting TNCs rather than for regulating them (see Chapters 3 and 5). As we learned in Chapter 3, the efforts of the G77 and Sweden to push a code forward through the UNCTC prior to UNCED came to nothing, and the UNCTC was disbanded. The objectives of that code would have been a good starting point for current efforts, as it would have required corporations to 'respect worker rights, to stop bribing public officials, to disclose potential dangers of products and production processes and carry out a

number of other obligations in exchange for government promises of equitable treatment to foreign firms' (Barnet and Cavanagh, 1994: 186).

Over the long term, the alternative vision for a mandatory global code would go much further. The ultimate goal of the alternative approach is to move to a situation where TNCs barely matter, as economies will be organised around 'institutions anchored in, and accountable to, the local community' (Korten, 1995: 312). Korten has suggested that a UN Regulatory Agency for Transnational Trade and Investment (UNRATTI) would be an appropriate host for a global code. The design is very different indeed to the voluntary Global Compact promoted by UN Secretary-General Kofi Annan, which was examined in Chapter 6. The ultimate objective of UNRATTI would be to promote local self-reliance and global equity, and to that end its role would help governments develop and enforce agreements relating to TNCs (Korten, 1995: 324). Korten argues that this body could help citizens work to remove corporations from the political space, which citizenry alone must rightly occupy. It is not the job of corporations to be involved in the political process, global, national or local. The code would empower national governments to set the rules for the entry and participation of corporations in the national arena. The basic principle to be followed would be this: 'when TNCs participate in a local economy they come only as invited guests, not as occupying forces, and are expected to honour local rules and customs' (Korten, 1995: 322).

Trade: Making it Fair

What we should seek is a framework within which all peoples of the North and the South, the East and the West, can trade fairly without oppression or exploitation. For we all share one world, the planet earth. (Brown, 1993: 11)

The alternative proposals for trade are based on the belief that the world trading system is characterised by unfair, unequal exchange, and that trade must be made to work for people. This will necessitate giving governments a central role. Herman Daly argues that governments must be free to chose not to trade and to pursue self-sufficiency if they have a mandate from citizens to take that path. If governments follow trade liberalisation, then they must decide the appropriate pace. Should a liberalisation path be favoured, then a redistributive mechanism should be put in place to compensate those states that lose out under the pursuit of global advantage (Daly, 1998). For example, this would help Third World countries adversely affected by the introduction of labour or environmental standards (see Chapter 6). As we progress toward these long-term trade goals, contributory steps can be taken along the way. Fair trade and ethical trade provide examples of such steps already in operation.

Fair trade

Fair trade is a special method of trading which supporters of the alternative approach would like to see become the standard method. It is based on the premise that it simply isn't fair that so many people world-wide live in poverty and uncertainty while working hard to produce commodities for consumption elsewhere. Fair trade works to ensure a better deal for small-scale, independent producers who have been marginalised by international trading and have often been vulnerable to unscrupulous middlemen. As such, fair trade is complementary to ethical trade, which is designed to help improve the working conditions of waged employees – see <www.co-op.co.uk/Ext_1/Development>.

The Fairtrade Foundation has developed a Fairtrade Mark that is attributed to individual products, which meet set criteria. These are shown in Box 7.1.

Box 7.1: The Fairtrade Foundation's Charter

This Charter sets out the principles for responsible sourcing of products from Third World Countries. The Charter stands for:

- Buying from responsible producers or suppliers, who provide fair remuneration and conditions of employment, including the right to organise
- Paying a fair price, which reflects the costs of production and quality of the product plus a margin for investment and development
- Providing financial credit where necessary to protect the producer against production uncertainties and financial exploitation
- Encouraging equal rewards for women and men
- Identifying and encouraging environmentally sustainable production
- Establishing stable trading relationships on the basis of quality, continuity and mutual support.

Source: cited in Brown, 1993: 183.

The example of coffee illustrates why fair trade is so important to human security (see Box 7.2). The Fairtrade Foundation's report, *Spilling the Beans*, makes chilling reading (Fairtrade Foundation, 1997). The report notes that coffee is grown by around 10 million farmers, 7 million of whom are smallholders with less than five hectares of land. From tree to supermarket shelf, the report estimates that the coffee beans change hands perhaps 150 times. The producers earn very little for their beans. Moreover, fluctuations in the price of the commodity hits small farmers very hard, and often means that their returns are less than the cost of production. Often they get into debt in order to grow the coffee. Coffee fairly traded offers these growers an opportunity to exist above mere subsistence level. However, unfair trade means that often trade causes harm not good. The report shows that this is true not only at the household level of individual farmers, but also at the country level. Some countries, such as Burundi and Uganda, depend on coffee for over 75 per cent of their export earnings, while others, such as Nicaragua and Tanzania, depend on it for over 20 per cent. Without some stability in price and market, development planning is severely limited.

Box 7.2: Fairtrade Foundation's basic principles of Fairtrade coffee

Fairtrade coffees are bought directly from democratic small farmer organisations under terms of trade which include:

- A fair price, one that covers the cost of production, a basic living wage and allows a margin above the market for social or environmental investment.
- Up to 60 per cent of the contract value available as credit so the producers can finance the purchase and shipment
- Long-term trading contracts in order to help farmers plan the year's exports and thus do not have to sell quickly at a low price.

Source: Fairtrade Foundation, 1997: 12.

Currently 240 farmers' organisations, representing half a million peasant coffee growers, are on the Fairtrade Register. For these growers and their families, the difference between fair trade and free trade is the difference between human security and insecurity. Consider the issue of credit: the Fairtrade study on coffee reported that lack of access to credit on favourable rates is one of the most important factors undermining small farmers:

> Without loans at a *decent rate of interest*, it is impossible for farmers to ensure adequate care for their crops, or to look after their families before harvest. After harvest, the need to clear punitive debts leads them to sell their crop quickly to the first trader, just when prices are low. Shortage of credit also undermines the attempts of farmers to set up collectives schemes to by-pass the middlemen, since the coops themselves lack the finance to buy the crop, fertiliser, equipment or expertise. (Fairtrade Foundation, 1997: 10; emphasis added)

While this comment is made in relation to coffee, the issue of access to favourable credit is equally important across the whole raft of commodities produced by small farmers for export. The climate of neoliberalism has narrowed the type of credit options for peasants across the globe (see Chapter 3). With the closure of government-financed credit institutions, small farmers are ever more at the mercy of unscrupulous moneylenders and market-rate microfinance.

Fairtrade products occupy a rapidly expanding niche market in developed countries, for example, Fairtrade coffee occupies 3 per cent of the UK market. This is very small, but has been achieved in a short time-frame. Many consumers are prepared to pay a premium above the market price to purchase products traded in a fairer manner.

Ethical trade
The Ethical Trading Initiative brings together independent interested parties such as NGOs, trade unions, retailers and suppliers to establish consistent standards on ethical trading principles. Some companies are already following their own such initiative. In the UK, the Co-op provides an excellent example. Concerned about the exploitation of workers, the Co-op wanted to encourage and support employers 'to ensure basic human and labour rights, develop and improve safe and decent working conditions, and improve general standards of living'. Moreover, it wanted to see if it could do this without adding a price premium to products. The Co-op enjoys the distinction of offering the first mainstream grocery product to be sourced and marketed on the basis of an ethical trading approach: Co-op 99 Tea. The Co-op has declared publicly that it 'is committed to ensuring that one day all Co-op brand products meet the standards of sound sourcing' – see <www.co-op.co.uk/Ext_1/Development>.

Fair trade and ethical trade represent small but none the less significant steps on the road to a different way of trading. They are important also because they demonstrate what can be done by individuals working together in developed countries to improve the security of households in other parts of the world with whom they are linked, not just by the global economy but by the feeling of shared humanity.

Finance

> The almost total freedom given to international investors and speculators has wreaked financial and now economic and social chaos. The time has now come to regulate these big players. (Khor, 1999b)

The alternative approach to finance is based on the belief that capital must work for the majority of people directly, and this must be secured by public regulation and redistribution. Capital must be predominantly productive rather than speculative, and long term rather than short term. Ideally, finance should be public rather than private. If its origin can be local, all the better, as this will ensure a stake in the local community. Most definitely, it will need to be *publicly regulated*. Capital can be made to work for people in various ways, and here we consider a representative selection: the role of national regulation, regional associations and a global redistributive mechanism commonly known as the 'Tobin tax'.

National regulation

The alternative approach, supported by UNCTAD's *Trade and Development Report* (1998), argues that at the national level, governments should be allowed regulate capital with a view to protecting national economies and citizens from the adverse effects of highly mobile short-term capital and currency speculation (Khor, 1999b). Capital controls are regarded as legitimate policy instruments, with a proven track record for dealing with volatile capital flows. Indeed, for Prime Minister Mahatir of Malaysia, any actions short of currency control are purely cosmetic. This position goes against conventional neoclassical economic theory and the wishes of the IMF and World Bank.

A few countries have utilised short-term capital controls, such as Poland, Chile and India (Reinventing Bretton Woods Committee, 1999). However, the Malaysian government has been the most vocal advocate. In September 1998, it introduced the following measures:

- The Central Bank of Malaysia pegged the Malaysian ringgit at 3.80 to the US$.
- Overseas dealing in the ringgit was prohibited.

- Malaysian residents were restricted in the amounts of money they could take out of the country, and also in the purposes for which it could be taken out.
- The capital and profits of foreign investors were to be locked into the Malaysian market for a year. (Khor, 1999a, 1999b)

These controls were eased at the beginning of February 1999, with a graduated levy, or exit tax, on foreign investments in Malaysian stock (Stewart, 1999). The Malaysian government claims that these measures have contributed to an increase in reserves, an improved current account balance and a balance of trade surplus. It presents the measures as the 'only reasonable option for Malaysia, or any small country who finds its currency under attack' (Malaysian Government, 1999: xiv). In a surprising move, the World Bank lent qualified support for Malaysian measures (Global Intelligence Update, 1999). However, an IMF study of capital controls in 14 countries, in January 2000, argued simply that they 'may have benefits as well as costs' (Aslam 2000; *World Bank Development News*, 12 January 2000).

Regional action

Regional action can be taken to help protect countries against problems associated with financial liberalisation. The East Asian crisis, and the IMF handling of it, has stimulated ideas about the possibility of an Asian regional bloc to deal with capital and currency matters. At the time of the crisis, Japan proposed an Asian Monetary Fund (AMF), but this idea was dismissed by the IMF and Western powers.

Former Japanese Vice-Finance Minister Eisuke Sakakibara is fearful that global financial markets have changed little since the crisis in 1997, and therefore the risk of disruptive capital flows remains high (*World Bank Development News*, 15 February 2000). He has called for an Asian currency regime to be developed to stabilise exchange rates in the region (*World Bank Development News*, 12 January 2000). This would institute regional capital controls. Also he identifies the need for a regional lender of last resort to mobilise regional savings to defend regional markets.

Asian confidence in the ability of the IMF to deal with another crisis in an acceptable manner remains low. South East Asian finance ministers, meeting in Brunei in March 2000, discussed the AMF, but could not agree on the mechanisms for its establishment. Malaysia, for example, is not keen on the AMF being tied too closely to Japan, and would like to see it housed elsewhere in the region. Prime Minister Mahatir has suggested that countries would contribute to the fund according to their ability, and they could call on it in time of real financial need.

The IMF and the Western states continue to oppose an AMF, but opinions differ as to why this is so. The IMF says that South East Asian nations are not yet ready for an AMF. However, one senior Singaporean banker believes that 'The west, and the IMF in particular, is worried about losing influence and leverage in the region if an AMF is established. They want to be able to continue to dictate to governments how to handle monetary crises' (Aglionby, 2000). It is probably only a matter of time before the region has its own monetary fund.

Global action: an international speculation tax
Redistributive mechanisms are one way of making finance work for people. One example is a campaign underway for a speculation tax on the world's major currencies to discourage short-term capital movements (Stecher with Bailey, 1999). The idea of a tax on international currency transactions was proposed in the late 1970s by Professor James Tobin of Yale University (Anderson et al., 1998) and developed further in 1996 by the German economist Paul Bernd Spahn. The group, Tobin Tax Initiative USA, describes the tax as a proposal 'to tax cross-border currency transactions, for the purpose of reining in market volume and volatility; restoring national sovereignty over monetary policy; and raising substantial revenue for urgent global environmental and human needs' (Tobin Tax Initiative, USA, 2000).

The 'Tobin tax', as it has come to be known, would place a small tax, from about 0.1 per cent to 0.25 per cent on all foreign exchange transactions, and would have the effect of reducing short-term movements of money. The tax would reduce the incentive for short-term currency speculation by rising in inverse proportion to the turn-around period. About US$ 1.8 trillion dollars a day was being exchanged in international currency deals in 1998, compared with US$ 200 billion in 1986: '... in less than a week, foreign exchange transactions exceed the entire annual volume of world trade in goods and services' (Discussion Draft, January 25, 2000, US House 'Tobin Tax' Resolution, Congressman Peter DeFazio, D-OR). The tax would be quite lucrative. The money yielded from it – a projected US$ 50 billion to US$ 300 billion a year – could potentially be used in civil sectors such as health and education.

The success of the Tobin tax campaign network is seen in the fact that parliamentary discussions on the tax, which began in Canada in March 1999, spread to the UK, France and the EU later that year, and then to Germany, Switzerland and Finland. The campaign continues.

The Tobin tax represents the beginning of the process of trans-formation. Thereafter, Chossudovsky calls for 'financial disarmament', which would involve:

> ... freezing (nationally and internationally) the entire gamut of speculative instruments, dismantling the hedge funds, reintroducing controls on the international movement of money and progressively breaking down the structures of offshore banking which provide a safe haven to 'dirty money' and the flight of undeclared corporate profits. (Chossudovsky, 1998)

Such measures would require a completely different global governance structure to that currently operating. Public regulation of finance is at the core of the alternative vision; this is in direct contrast to the reformist vision. Recall that Alan Greenspan believes private finance is too complex for public regulation (see Chapter 6).

Democratising Global Governance

The alternative path requires a continuous evolution towards more inclusive, bottom-up, participatory politics. The ultimate goal is participatory local democracy that will enable people to exert far greater control over their own lives than at present. While direct citizen participation at the global level is not practically feasible at present, the global level of governance can nevertheless be constructed along far more participatory lines by the involvement of more states in meaningful decision making. This would have the knock-on effect of changing the mandate of these institutions.

It is important at this juncture to stress the expansion of *state involvement* in global governance. The reason is that a standard reformist response to the call for broadening participation is to widen the involvement of civil society. Hence Ruggiero, as Director-General of the WTO, called for more civil society involvement given that trade rules are increasingly affecting day-to-day lives. For advocates of the alternative approach, however, increased pluralism such as this does not address the fundamental problem of the structure of social power in the organisation: who sets the agenda, and in whose interests? While there is a role for civil society groups, they too are unelected representatives of citizenry. In contrast, national governments are mandated to represent citizens, they are accountable to citizens and they are responsible for the human security of citizens. They must be able to exercise judgements with the goal of human security in mind. They must be able to make the case for developmental and social imperatives in all international fora, confident that they will be heard and that their voices will count.

This broadening of state-level representation in global governance is desirable for a number of reasons: first, it is regarded as fair; second, it will help advance the quality of those institutions' processes, in terms of factors such as openness, accountability and transparency; third, it will result in a change in the focus of interest of the organisations in the direction of a more human-centred development. This of course is provided that states themselves have developed better mechanisms for participation within their domestic political structures.

Regarding fairness, as we saw in Chapter 1, many sceptics regard the IFIs as being over-determined by the US, and within the US, over-determined by the inclinations of the US Treasury, acting on behalf of Wall Street bankers. The US is the largest contributor and largest quota holder in the IMF. Dependence on Congressional appropriations gives the US a very high degree of leverage over policies, loan conditionality and leadership matters.

But the power of the US and Western states does not originate in the veto; rather it is reflected in the veto. The power is of a structural nature. The veto does not need to be used; its existence encourages consensus. Majority membership of an organisation is no guarantee of influence. Developing countries are in a majority at the WTO, but this does not mean that they can exert significant influence on the trade agenda or on outcomes. What matters is not the exercise of numerical strength, but rather the exercise of social power (Wilkin, 2000). Decisions are made in the WTO by the 'consensus of the Quad', that is, the US, Europe, Japan and Canada. This was exemplified in the Seattle summit, in the exclusive 'Green Room meetings' which did not have the mandate of the full membership, which were not officially announced, and the results of which were generally not made known (Khor, 2000a, 2000b). Developing countries form a majority of the membership of the WTO, and their citizens form the majority of global citizens. Global governance institutions must provide them the proper opportunity to participate meaningfully in debate and decision making.

The leaders of the IFIs enjoy very significant unelected power, especially so in the case of the IMF. The alternative approach seeks to erode this power, to chip away at it. For example, they would like to see new rules for the election of the Managing Director of the IMF and other IFIs. In place of the unspoken agreement that a European heads the IMF, and an American the World Bank, they would like to see an open selection process. In order for that to occur, 'deep reforms of the entire organisation' will be necessary (Calomaris, 2000). Recent protracted European foot-dragging over the choice of Camdessus's successor at least opened the political space for a discussion of these matters. Given the changes being mooted by reformers in the function of the IMF, it would not be unreasonable for the post to go to a candidate from an emerging market economy. However, this has not happened.

The IMF is not alone in these problems. Unpleasant wrangling over the choice of WTO Director-General Ruggiero's successor has raised concerns over lack of transparency and democracy in the decision-making machinery of the WTO (see Raghavan, 1999).

Regarding improving the quality of governance processes, the alternative approach envisages the IFIs applying the same standards of good governance internally as they expect of client states. They would like to see an effective, transparent, independent evaluation mechanism, which would make it easier to bring the IFIs to account if they were failing in their job. Several NGOs have been campaigning vigorously over the last decade for such reform of the IMF, including the Center of Concern in Washington DC, the Bretton Woods project in London and many others. With the exception of the extremely limited external evaluation process initiated in 1996, evaluation of IMF lending has been conducted in-house. Most of that has not been open to public scrutiny, for example, the 1998 review of the IMF's handling of the Indonesian crisis. Campaigners are calling for a properly funded evaluation unit, with independent staff (Wood and Welch, 2000). Independent monitoring would be essential to reveal how far the recommendations of such a unit were being implemented by the institution.

While there has been some small opening of what is essentially a highly closed and secretive organisation, there is still a very long way to go and much resistance, not only by IMF staff but also by many governments. UK Minister of Finance Gordon Brown, for example, when questioned by the Treasury Select Committee in December 1999, refused to confirm or deny the UK's voting position on a large loan to Russia. He said that he wanted the international financial community to move together on the issue of openness, and that to date many countries are cautious (Wood, 1999).

The change in focus of the IFIs that would automatically ensue from wider and *more meaningful* state-level participation in global-level decision making is exemplified by the experience of the WTO agenda. If the trade regime were to embrace all members in an equitable fashion, then its agenda would look very different. Trade liberalisation would not be valued in itself, and growth would not be the primary goal. Other values would be reflected on the trade agenda, particularly those pertaining to the development concerns of the majority of states.

Third World states fear that the First World states are driving the WTO agenda at a speed and in a direction that pays insufficient attention to the interests of the majority of many member states, and to the interests of the majority of the global population (WTO, 1999: 2–3). Thus if they exerted meaningful influence in the institution, the development needs of the majority of WTO members would be placed at the top of the organisation's agenda and mainstreamed in its work. Recognition of the special and different nature of developing countries would result in systematic special and different treatment.

The primary task for developing countries now in the WTO is to review the existing system in a realistic time-frame, and to work to change it where it is seen to result in inequities. Many developing countries simply don't have the capacity to quickly figure out the implications of trade rules that the developed countries are keen to push ahead. They need time to work out what is in their best interests and to negotiate with this in mind. The Chairman of the G77 therefore argues that the biannual Ministerial meeting should be replaced by a five-yearly meeting which would allow more time for proper reflection on the trade matters at hand (cited in Khor, 2000c).

In this context, the collapse of the Seattle meeting may be seen as an opportunity for the advocates of the alternative approach, embracing Third World states and civil society groups in South and North. They can push for the sort of multilateral trading institution and the type of trading system that they feel more effectively meet human needs.

Conclusion

Advocates of the alternative path, while believing that very significant changes to global development policy are needed to effect global redistribution, are willing as a first step to advocate the sort of changes in trade, finance, investment and governance explored above. The widespread adoption of these policies would begin the process of addressing the deepening global crisis of inequality and poverty. For them, therefore, the alternative pathway is actually the path to stability, peace and human security. The measures they suggest, however, lie outside of the reformist development pathway presently being carved out by global governance institutions. However, the measures suggested by the alternative approach are hardly radical in themselves; they are still working within the current order, but with the long-term goal of transformation.

Reformists accept that life is unfair (Birdsall, 1998), but exponents of the alternative approach argue that it doesn't have to be. Susan George's words, cited earlier, are well worth repeating here: 'Neoliberalism is not a force like gravity, but an artificial construct' (George, 1999a). Current choices are very significant. These choices are being made by unrepresentative global governance institutions, by a handful of states, by increasingly powerful corporate actors and by the 20 per cent of the world's population who exercise consumer choice in the global market-place (see Table 7.1).

Table 7.1: The world's priorities? (annual expenditure, in US$ billion)

Basic education for all	6*
Cosmetics in the US	8
Water and sanitation for all	9*
Ice cream in Europe	11
Reproductive health for all women	12*
Perfumes in Europe and the US	12
Basic health and nutrition	13*
Pet foods in Europe and US	17
Business entertainment in Japan	35
Cigarettes in Europe	50
Alcoholic drinks in Europe	105
Narcotic drugs in the world	400
Military spending in the world	780

* Estimated additional annual cost to achieve universal access to basic social services in all developing countries.

Source: UNDP, 1998: 37.

We can make different choices. And we will. One commentator has remarked that 'It will be citizen movements creating pressure on governments and directly on corporations that will be central in the creation of ... mechanisms to promote corporate accountability' (Cavanagh, 1997: 103). A new, mandatory type of business practice will ensue. Beyond that, a new type of participatory politics will ensue, and a more appropriate agenda for meeting human security will be developed. The role of citizens as agents of this change – that is, the role of me and you and us – should not be underestimated.

References and Bibliography

Adams, N. (1993) *Worlds Apart: The North–South Divide and the International System* (London: Zed Books).

African Development Bank (1998) *African Development Bank Report* (Oxford: Oxford University Press).

Aglionby, J. (2000) 'Asia shelves IMF Challenge', *Guardian* (London), 27 March.

Allen, T. and Thomas, A. (1992) *Poverty and Development in the 1990s* (Oxford: Oxford University Press).

Amoako, K. (1999), 'Press statement of Executive Secretary K.Y. Amoako at the UN ECA conference' (Addis Ababa: ECA) 6 May.

Anderson, S., Barry, T. and Honey, M. (1998) 'International Financial Flows', *Foreign Policy in Focus*, 3, 41.

Andor, L. and Summers, M. (1998) *Market Failure: Eastern Europe's Economic Miracle* (London: Pluto Press).

Annan, K. (1999) 'The Secretary-General's Address to the World Economic Forum', UN press release, 31 January.

Aslam, Abid (2000) 'Confessions of the Washington Ideologues: Analysis', Inter Press Service, Washington DC, 14 January.

Axworthy, L. (1997) 'Canada and human security: the need for leadership', *International Journal*, L11: 2 (Spring), pp. 183–96.

Bain, W. (1999) 'Against Crusading: The Ethic of Human Security and Canadian Foreign Policy', *Canadian Foreign Policy*, 6:3, pp. 85–98.

Bank Information Center (1999) 'Headlines of the 1999 World Bank/IMF Annual Meetings', Bank Information Center, October (Washington, DC: World Bank).

Barker, D. and Mander, J. (2000) 'Invisible Government', *Third World Resurgence*, 112/113, January, p. 37.

Barnet, R. and Cavanagh, J. (1994) 'A Global New Deal', in J. Cavanagh, D. Wysham, and M. Arruda (eds) *Beyond Bretton Woods* (London: Pluto Press), chapter 15.

Barya, J. (1993) 'The new politcal conditionalities of aid: an independent view from Africa', *IDS Bulletin*, 26:1, pp. 16–23.

Beck, U. (1992) *Risk Society* (London: Sage).

Beder, S. (1997) *Global Spin: The Corporate Assault on Environmentalism* (Devon: Green Books).

Bello, W. (1994) *Dark Victory: The US, Structural Adjustment and Global Poverty* (London: Pluto Press).

Bello, W. (1997) 'Fast-track capitalism, geoeconomic competition and the sustainable development-challenge in East Asia', in C. Thomas and P. Wilkin (eds) *Globalisation and the South* (Basingstoke: Macmillan), pp. 143–62.

Bello, W. (1999) 'The TNC World Order: Will it Also Unravel?', paper prepared for the Democracy, Market Economy and Development conference, Seoul, Korea, 26–27 February.

Bhagwati, J. (1998) 'The capital myth; the difference between trade in widgets and dollars', *Foreign Affairs*, May/June, 77:3, pp. 7–17.

Bird, G. and Killick, T. (1995) *The Bretton Woods Institutions: A Commonwealth Perspective* (London: Commonwealth Secretariat).

Birdsall, N. (1998) 'Life is Unfair: Inequality in the World', *Foreign Policy*, Summer, pp. 76–93.

Broad, R. and Landi, C. M. (1996) 'Whither the North–South Gap?', *Third World Quarterly*, 17:1, pp. 7–17.

Brown, L. R. and Kane, H. (1995) *Full House: Reassessing the Earth's Population Carrying Capacity* (London: Earthscan).

Brown, M. (1993) *Fair Trade* (London: Zed Books).

Brown, M. (1995) *Africa's Choices* (London: Penguin).

Brown, M. (1996) 'Aid Moves from the Messianic to the Managerial', *The World Today*, June, pp. 157–9.

Calomaris, C. (2000) 'IMF Needs More than a New Boss', *Wall Street Journal*, 2 March.

Camdessus, M. (2000a) 'Videoteleconference with press before meeting of the African Heads of State, 34th OAU Summit, Gabon', IMF press release, 18–19 January.

Camdessus, M. (2000b) 'Address to the tenth UNCTAD, 13 February', *World Bank Development News*, 14 February.

Camdessus, M. (2000c) 'Poverty Reduction and Growth: An Agenda for Africa at the Dawn of the Third Millennium' Opening Remarks at the Summit Meeting of African Heads of State, Libreville, Gabon, 18 January.

Capdevila, G. (1999) 'Human Rights Body to Scrutinise TNC Activities', August <www.twnside.org.sg/south/twn/title/hr_cn.htm>

Cavanagh, J. (1997) 'Rethinking Corporate Accountability', in J. Griesgraber and B. Gunter (eds) *World Trade: Towards Fair and Free Trade in the Twenty-first Century* (London: Pluto Press), pp. 91–107.

Cavanagh, J., Wysham, D. and Arruda, M. (eds) (1994) *Beyond Bretton Woods* (London: Pluto Press).

Chandler, G. (1999) 'Doing the Right Thing', *Green Futures*, March/April, pp. 22–3.

Chatterjee, P. and Finger, M. (1994) *The Earth Brokers* (London: Routledge).

Chossudovsky, M. (1997) *The Globalization of Poverty: Impacts of IMF and World Bank Reforms* (London: Zed Books).

Chossudovsky, M. (1998) 'The G7 "Solution" to the Global Financial Crisis: A Marshall Plan for Creditors and Speculators' (University of Ottawa: Department of Economics).

Chossudovsky, M. (1999) 'Human security and economic genocide in Rwanda', in C. Thomas and P. Wilkin (eds) *Globalization, Human Security and the African Experience* (Colorado: Lynne Reinner), pp. 117–26.

Chote, R. (1999) 'Forum to help prevent crises agreed', *Financial Times*, London, 22 February.

Clapham, C. (1998) 'Degrees of Statehood', *Review of International Studies*, 24, pp. 143–57.

Clark, J. (1991) *Democratizing Development: The Role of Voluntary Organizations* (London: Earthscan).

Committee of Inquiry (1999) *A New Vision for Business* (London: Forum for the Future).

The Co-operative Bank (1997) *The Partnership Report* (Manchester: The Co-operative Bank).

Corner House (1998) *The Myth of the Minimalist State*, Briefing No. 5 (Dorset, UK: Corner House).

Cornia, A., Jolly, R. and Stewart, F. (1987) *Adjustment with a Human Face* (Oxford: Oxford University Press).

Cox, R. (1999) 'Civil Society at the turn of the millennium: prospects for an alternative world order', *Review of International Studies*, 25:1, pp. 3–28.

Crossette, B. (1996) 'UN survey finds rich–poor gap widening', *New York Times*, 15 July, p. 55.

Daly, H. (1998) 'Globalization versus Internationalization: Some Implications', November, available from School of Public Affairs, University of Maryland, College Park, MD 20742–1821, US.

Davies, N. (1998) *Dark Heart: The Shocking Truth about Hidden Britain* (London: Vintage).

DeFazio, US Congressman P. (2000) 'US House Tobin Tax Resolution, Revised discussion draft 25 January 2000', *Tobin Tax Update*, January (US: Tobin Tax Initiative).

Development Initiatives (1997) *The Reality of Aid 1997/8* (London: Earthscan).

Development Initiatives (2000) *The Reality of Aid 2000* (London: Earthscan).

Dumont, R. (1966; 1988) *False Start in Africa* (London: Earthscan).

ECLAC (1997) 'Summary of global economic developments', *UN Focus in the Caribbean: Newsletter of the UN System in the Caribbean*, January–June, pp. 6–7.

Ekins, P. (1992) *A New World Order: Grassroots Movements for Global Change* (London: Routledge).

Elliott, L. (1997) 'World Warned of Poverty Time Bomb', *Guardian*, 24 September, p. 21.

Escobar, A. (1995) *Encountering Development: The Making and Unmaking of the Third World* (Princeton: Princeton University Press).

EU (1998) 'Improving the Transparency of WTO Operations', 13 July, sent to the WTO for circulation as WT/GC/W/92, 14 July.

EURODAD (2000) 'Comments on Upcoming Meltzer Commission Report', *EURODAD Comments*, 2 March.

Evans, T. (1996) *US Hegemony and the Project of Universal Human Rights* (Basingstoke: Macmillan).

Evans, T. (ed.) (1998) *Human Rights Fifty Years On: A Reappraisal* (Manchester: Manchester University Press).

Evans, T. (1999) 'Trading human rights', in A. Taylor and C. Thomas (eds) *Global Trade and Global Social Issues* (London: Routledge), pp. 31–52.

Fairtrade Foundation (1997) *Spilling the Beans: What's Wrong with the Coffee Trade* <www.gn.apc.org/faitrade/spilling1.htm>.

Falk, R. (1971) *This Endangered Planet* (New York: Random House).

Falk, R. (1975) *A Study of Future Worlds* (New York: The Free Press).

Falk, R. et al. (eds) (1991) *The United Nations and a Just World Order* (Boulder: Westview Press).

Feldstein, M. (1998) 'Refocusing the IMF', *Foreign Affairs*, March/April.

Fidler, S. (2000) 'Report urges slimming down of IMF and World Bank', *Financial Times*, 8 March.

Financial Times Management (1998) *Visions of Ethical Business*, No. 1, October (London: *Financial Times* Management).

Finger, M. and Lobina, E. (1999) 'Managing Trade in a Globalizing World: trade in public services and transnational corporations: the case of the global water industry', in A. Taylor and C. Thomas (eds) *Global Trade and Global Social Issues* (London: Routledge), pp. 170–96.

Forcese, C. (1997) *Commerce with Conscience* (Ottawa: ICHRDD).

FOE–US/TWN/IPS (Friends of the Earth US, Third World Network, Institute for Policy Studies, US) (1998) 'A Citizens' Agenda for Reform of the Global Economic System', alternatively referred to as 'The Declaration on the New Global Financial Architecture', FOE–US/TWN/IPS, December.

Fukuyama, F. (1989) 'The End of History', *The National Interest*, 16, pp. 3–18.

George, S. (1999a) 'A Short History of Neo-liberalism: Twenty Years of Elite Economics and Emerging Opportunities for Structural Change', paper presented at the Bangkok Conference on Economic Sovereignty, 24–26 March, <www.millennium-round.org/>.

George, S. (1999b) *The Lugano Report: On Preserving Capitalism in the Twenty-first Century* (London: Pluto Press).

Gill, S. (1995) 'Globalisation. Market Civilisation, and Disciplinary Neoliberalism', *Millennium*, 24:3, pp. 399–423.

Gillies, D. (1996) 'Human Rights, Democracy and Good Governance: Stretching the World Bank's Policy Frontiers', Chapter 5 in J. M. Griesgraber and B. Gunter (eds) *The World Bank* (London: Pluto Press), pp. 101–41.

Gills, B., Rocamora, J. and Wilson, R. (eds) (1993) *Low Intensity Democracy* (London: Pluto).

Global Intelligence Update (1999) 'World Bank Reverses Position on Financial Controls and on Malaysia', *Weekly Analysis*, 20 September.

Goldberg, M. (2000) 'China's New Emerging Micro Finance Industry', <www.cgap.org>.

Goldman, M. (ed.) (1998) *Privatising Nature* (London: Pluto Press).

Goozner, M. (1999) 'Poorest Nations Mired in Big Debt', *Chicago Tribune*, 19 March.

Griesgraber, J. and Gunter, B. (eds) (1997) *World Trade: Towards Fair and Free Trade in the Twenty-first Century* (London: Pluto Press).

Grinspun, R. and Cameron, M. (eds) (1993) *The Political Economy of North American Free Trade* (New York: St Martin's Press).

Guest, A. (1999) 'Security in the Senegal Basin', in C. Thomas and P. Wilkin, P. (eds) *Globalisation, Human Security and the African Experience* (Colorado: Lynne Reinner), pp. 101–16.

Hahnel, R. (1999) 'The Great Global Asset Swindle', *ZNet Commentary*, 23 March.

Hampson, F. O. and Oliver, D. F. (1998) 'Pulpit diplomacy: a critical assessment of the Axworthy doctrine', *International Journal*, L111:3, Summer, pp. 379–406.

Harbeson, J. W. (ed.) (1995) *Africa in World Politics* (Boulder: Westview Press).

The Harker Report (2000) *Human Security in the Sudan*, Canadian Department of Foreign Affairs website: <http://www.dfait-maeci.gc.ca/foreignp/menu-e.asp>.

Heinbecker, P. (1999) 'Human Security', *Headlines* (Toronto: Canadian Institute of International Affairs), 56:2, pp. 4–9.

Hobsbawn, E. (1995) *Age of Extremes: The Short Twentieth Century, 1914–1991* (London: Abacus).

Hogenboom, B. (1996) 'Cooperation and Polarisation Beyond Borders: the transnationalisation of Mexican environmental issues during the NAFTA negotiations', *Third World Quarterly*, 17:5, pp. 989–1005.

Hogenboom, B. (1998) *Mexico and the NAFTA Environment Debate* (International Books).

Hoogevelt, A. (1997) *Globalization and the Postcolonial World* (London: Macmillan).

Hulme, D. and Moseley, P. (1996) *Finance Against Poverty*, Volume 1 (London: Routledge).

The Hunger Project (1985) *Ending Hunger: An Idea Whose Time Has Come* (New York: Praeger).

Hurrell, A. and Woods, N. (1995) 'Globalisation and Inequality', *Millennium*, 24:3, pp. 447–70.

ICFTU (1999) *Building Workers' Human Rights into the Global Trading System* (Brussels: ICFTU).

ICPF (1994) *Uncommon Opportunities: An Agenda for Peace and Equitable Development* (London: Zed Books).

ICTSD (1998) 'NGO statement on WTO and transparency', July (Geneva: ICTSD).

International Trade Reporter (1999) 'Mulling Failed MAI Process, OECD Debates Future of Investment Liberalization Process' *International Trade Reporter*, 16:38, 29 September, p. 1570.

ILO (1998) *World Employment Report 1998–99* (Geneva: ILO).

Jackson, R. H. and Rosberg, C. G. (1982) 'Why Africa's Weak States Persist: the Empirical and the Juridical in Statehood', *World Politics*, 35:1, pp. 1–24.

Jackson, R. H. and Rosberg, C. G. (1986) 'Sovereignty and Underdevelopment: Juridical Statehood in the African Crisis', *Journal of Modern African Studies*, 24:1, pp. 1–31.

Jubilee 2000 Coalition Afrika Campaign (1999) 'Letter to members of the United States Congress', 11 March.

Justice, D. (1999) 'The new codes of conduct and the social partners', ICFTU, <www.icftu.org/english/tncs/glcindex.html>.

Kapur, D. (1998) 'The IMF: A Cure or a Curse?', *Foreign Policy*, 77:2, pp. 114–29.

Kegley, C. W. and Wittkopf, E. R. (1993) *World Politics: Trend and Transformation* (Basingstoke: Macmillan, 4th edn).

Kell, G. and Ruggie, J. G. (1999) 'Global Markets and Social Legitimacy: the case of the "Global Compact"', paper presented at the international conference, 'Governing the Public Domain beyond the Era of the Washington Consensus? Redrawing the Line Between the State and the Market', York University, Toronto, Canada, 4–6 November, available at <www.unglobalcompact.org/gc/unweb.nsf/content/gkjr.htm>.

Kende, I. (1971) 'Twenty Five Years of Local Wars', *Journal of Peace Research*, 8, pp. 5–22.

Key, S. (1999) 'Trade liberalization and prudential regulation: the international framework for financial services', *International Affairs*, 75:1, January, pp. 61–76.

Khor, M. (1996) 'Globalization: implications for development policy', *Third World Resurgence*, 74, pp. 15–22.

Khor, M. (1999a) 'Within the Third World, Malaysia's Case Could Help Ailing Brazil', *Third World Network Features*, 10 March.

Khor, M. (1999b) 'Why Capital Controls and International Debt Restructuring Mechanisms are Necessary to Prevent and Manage Financial Crises', June (Malaysia: Third World Network).

Khor, M. (2000a) 'Rethinking Liberalisation and Reforming the WTO', presentation at World Economic Forum, Davos, 28 January, on behalf of Third World Network, Malaysia.

Khor, M. (2000b) 'Initiate Reform of WTO, Says G77 Chairman', *Third World Resurgence*, 112/113, January, pp. 24–6.

Khor, M. (2000c) ''The revolt of developing nations', *Third World Resurgence*, 112/113, January, pp. 9–12.

Kidron, M. and Segal, R. (1987) *The New State of the World Atlas* (London and Sydney: Pan Books).

Killick, T. (1994) 'Structural Adjustment and Poverty Alleviation: An Interpretative Survey' (London: ODI), mimeo.

Korten, D. C. (1990) *Getting to the 21st Century: Voluntary Action and the Global Agenda* (Connecticut: Kumarian Press).

Korten, D. (1995) *When Corporations Rule the World* (London: Earthscan, reprinted 1997).

Kraus, J. (1999) 'Banks Rip IMF's Proposed Rules on Loans to Emerging Markets', *American Banker*, 21 September.

Krause, K. and Williams, M. C. (eds) (1997) *Critical Security Studies* (London: University College London Press).

Krugman, P. (1995) 'Dutch Tulips and Emerging Markets', *Foreign Affairs*, 74, pp. 28–44.

Lean, G. and Cooper, Y. (1996) 'The theory was that as the rich got richer, we'd all benefit, but it hasn't worked', *Independent on Sunday*, 21 July, pp. 52–3.

Leftwich, A. (1993) 'Governance, development and democracy in the Third World', *Third World Quarterly*, 14:3, pp. 605–24.

Leftwich, A. (1994) 'Governance, the State and the Politics of Development', *Development and Change*, 25, pp. 363–86.

LeQuesne, C. (1996) *Reforming World Trade: The Social and Environmental Priorities* (Oxford: Oxfam).

Luce, E. (1999) 'Brady Hits at IMF for "Playing with Fire"' *Financial Times*, 20 September.

McDonough, B. (1998) 'Issues for the Basle Accord', Federal Reserve Bank of New York, *Annual Report* (New York: FRB), pp. 3–12.

Madeley, J. (1999) *Big Business Poor Peoples: The Impact of Transnational Corporations on the World's Poor* (London: Zed Books).

Malaysian Government (1999) 'The Tiger Fights Back', *Financial Times*, London, 28 March.

Marlin, A. (1998) 'Visions of social accountability: SA8000', *Visions of Ethical Business*, No. 1, October (London: *Financial Times* Management).

Mayne, R. and LeQuesne, C. (1999) 'Cells for a Social Trade', in A. Taylor and C. Thomas (eds) *Global Trade and Global Social Issues* (London: Routledge), pp. 99–113.

Meltzer, A. (2000) *The International Financial Institution Advisory Commission* (or *The Meltzer Commission Report*) March (Washington, DC: US Congress).

Mendlovitz, S. (ed.) (1975) *On the Creation of a Just World Order* (New York: The Free Press).

Midgeley, M. (1992) 'Can science save its soul?', *New Scientist*, 1 August, pp. 24–7.

Mirza, Z. (2000) 'WTO must ensure access to medicines – HAI', *Third World Resurgence*, 112/113, January, p. 39.

Mosley, P., Harrigan, J. and Toye, J. (eds) (1991) *World Bank and Policy-Based Lending* (London: Routledge).

Neale, I. (1999) 'The WTO and issues associated with TRIPs and agrobiotechnology', chapter in A. Taylor and C. Thomas (eds) (1999) *Global Trade and Global Social Issues* (London: Routledge), pp. 114–32.

NGO statement (1998) 'Statement to the Secretary-General of UNCTAD by NGOs on the need to review UNCTAD's approach to a possible multilateral framework on investment', 11/12 June, Geneva, available from Martin Khor, Third World Network, Penang, Malaysia.

Norlen, D. and Thenard, E. (2000) 'Export Credit Agencies: The Hidden Agents of Corporate Globalization' February, <www.eca-watch.org>.

ODI (1996) 'Adjustment in Africa: Lessons from Ghana', ODI briefing paper, No. 3.

OECD (1996) 'OECD Employment Outlook', 9 July, SG/COM/PUN (96)65 (Paris: OECD).

OECD (1999) *Development Cooperation in the 1990s: Policy Statement by DAC Aid Ministers and Heads of Agencies* (Paris: OECD).

Ould-Mey, M. (1994) 'Global Adjustment: Implications for Peripheral States', *Third World Quarterly*, 15:2, pp. 319–36.

Oxfam International (1999) *Education Now, Break the Cycle of Poverty* (Oxford: Oxfam).

Panos Institute (1999) *Globalisation and Employment*, Briefing No. 33 (London: Panos Institute).

Pasha, M. (1996), 'Security as Hegemony', *Alternatives*, 21:3, July–September, pp. 283–302.

Phillips, M. (2000) 'Panel Assails IMF, World Bank Policies, says Institutions Failed Developing World', *Wall Street Journal*, 7 March.

Van der Pijl, K. (1998) *Transnational Classes and International Relations* (London: Routledge)

Pilger, J. (2000) 'Don't be Fooled by Debt Relief', *Guardian*, 10 January.

Porritt, J. (2000) 'Vision On?', *Green Futures*, January/February, pp. 44–5.

Pursey, S. (1998) 'Multinational Enterprises and the World of Work: Globalisation with a Human Face', article on the 20th Anniversary of the ILO Declaration on Multinational Enterprises and Social Policy, June, <www.icftu.org/english/tncs98ilo.html>.

Pye-Smith, C. and Feyerabend, G.B. (1994) *The Wealth of Communities* (London: Earthscan).

Raghavan, C. (1997) 'A New Trade Order in a World of Disorder', in J. Griesgraber and B. Gunter (eds) *World Trade: Towards Fair and Free Trade in the Twenty-first Century* (London: Pluto Press).

Raghavan, C. (1998) 'Globalization's political economy and state role', *South–North Development Monitor*, 15 July, Geneva.

Raghavan, C. (1999) 'Trade: From Rule-based to Rule-less System?', *South–North Development Monitor*, 4, 6, 7 and 10 May, Geneva.

Raghavan, C. (2000) 'Developing Nations Reject Labour issues in WTO', *Third World Resurgence*, January, pp. 29–31.

Rahnema, M. and Bawtree, V. (eds) (1997) *The Post Development Reader* (London: Zed Books).

Randel, J., German, T. and Ewing, D. (eds) (2000) *The Reality of Aid 2000: An Independent Review of Poverty Reduction and*

Development Assistance (London: Development Alternatives/ Earthscan/Reality of Aid Project).

Rapely, J. (1996) *Understanding Development* (Boulder: Lynne Rienner).

Reinventing Bretton Woods Committee (1999) 'An International Economic Challenge: the Complexity of Capital Mobility', First Report of the Reinventing Bretton Woods Committee on the Process Towards a New Financial Architecture (Canberra: Australian National University), 14 July.

Renner, M. (1997) *Fighting for Survival: Environmental Decline, Social Conflict and the New Age of Insecurity* (London: Earthscan).

Riley, S. P. and Parfitt, T. W. (1994) 'Economic Adjustment and Democratization in Africa', in J. Walton and D. Seddon, *Free Markets and Food Riots: the Politics of Global Adjustment* (Oxford: Blackwell), pp. 135–70.

Roberts, G. (1984) *Questioning Development* (London: Returned Volunteer Action).

Ross, A. (ed.) (1997) *No Sweat: Fashion, Free Trade and the Rights of Garment Workers* (London: Verso).

Rowntree Foundation (1995) *Inquiry into Income and Wealth* (York: Joseph Rowntree Foundation).

Rubin, US Treasury Secretary (1999) 'Remarks on the Reform of the International Financial Architecture to the School of Advanced Studies', Princeton University, 21 April.

Sachs, J. (1998) 'Stop Preaching', *Financial Times*, London edn 1, 5 November.

Samuel, J. (2000) 'The Holy Cow of Microcredit', *Third World Resurgence*, No. 112/113 (December 1999/January 2000).

Saurin, J. (1996), 'Globalization, Poverty and the Promise of Modernity', *Millennium*, 25:3, pp. 657–80.

Saurin, J. (1997) 'Organising Hunger: the Global Organization of Famines and Feasts', in C. Thomas and P. Wilkin, (eds) *Globalization and the South* (London: Macmillan), pp. 106–23.

Saurin, J. (1999) 'The global production of trade and social movements: value, regulation, effective demand and needs', in A. Taylor and C. Thomas (eds) *Global Trade and Global Social Issues* (London: Routledge), pp. 217–35.

Scholte, J. A. (1997) 'Global Trade and Finance', in J. Bayles and S. Smith (eds) *The Globalization of World Politics* (Oxford: Oxford University Press), pp. 429–48.

Schumacher, E. F. (1973) *Small is Beautiful: Economics as if People Mattered* (New York: Harper and Row).

Shaw, T. and Quadir, F. (1997) 'Democratic Development in the South in the Next Millennium: What prospects for Avoiding Anarchy and Authoritarianism?', in C. Thomas and P. Wilkin (eds) *Globalization and the South* (London: Macmillan), pp. 36–59.

Shiva, V. (1995) 'Indian farmers protest against pro-liberalisation agricultural policy', *Third World Resurgence*, December, pp. 33–5.

Shrybman, S. (1992) 'Trading Away the Environment', *World Policy Journal*, 9, pp. 93–110.

Shuman, M. (1994) 'Lilliputian Power: A World Economy As if Communities Mattered', in J. Cavanagh, D. Wysham and M. Arruda (eds) *Beyond Bretton Woods* (London: Pluto Press), pp. 181–201.

Sinclair, T. (1994) 'Between State and Market: Hegemony and Institutions of Collective Action under Conditions of International Capital Mobility', *Policy Sciences*, 27:4, pp. 447–66.

Smith, D. (1997) *The State of War and Peace Atlas* (London: Penguin).

South Commission (1990) *The Challenge to the South* (Oxford: Oxford University Press).

Speth, J.G. (1996) in *New York Times*, 15 July, p. 55.

Stecher, H. with Bailey, M. (1999) 'Time for a Tobin Tax? Some Practical and Political Arguments', Oxfam Discussion Paper, Oxfam GB Policy Department, Oxford.

Stephens, L. (1998) 'Between NAFTA and Zapata: Responses to Restructuring the Commons in Chiapas and Oaxaca, Mexico', in Goldman, M. (ed.) *Privatising Nature* (London: Pluto Press).

Stewart, I. (1999) 'Malaysia Loosens Capital Controls', *The Australian News*, 5 February.

Stiglitz, J. (1998) 'More Instruments and Broader Goals: Moving Toward the Post-Washington Consensus', WIDER Annual Lectures, No. 2 (Helsinki: United Nations University).

Stiglitz, J. (1999) 'Whither Reform? Ten Years of the Transition', keynote address at the Annual World Bank Conference on Development Economics, Washington, DC, 28–30 April.

Stone, J. (2000) *Losing Perspective* (London: International Broadcasting Trust).

Subbarao, K. et al. (1997) *Safety Net Programs and Poverty Reduction: Lessons from Cross- Country Experience* (Washington, DC: World Bank).

Summers, L. (1999) 'The Right Kind of IMF for a Stable Global Financial System', US Treasury Secretary's Remarks to the London School of Business, UK (Washington, DC Treasury News from the Office of Public Affairs, US Treasury), 14 December.

Summers, L. (2000) 'Personal View: The Troubling Aspects of IMF Reform', *Financial Times*, 23 March.

Tandon, Y. (2000) 'Defining Development in the WTO', *SEATINI Bulletin*, International South Group Network <saetini.zw@unpd.org>.

Taylor, A. and Thomas, C (eds) (1999) *Global Trade and Global Social Issues* (London: Routledge).

Thatcher, M. (1996) 'Geographical Society Presidential Dinner Address', *Independent on Sunday*, 21 July, p. 52.

Thomas, A. et al. (1994) *Third World Atlas* (Milton Keynes: Open University Press, 2nd edn).

Thomas, C. (1985) *New States, Sovereignty and Intervention* (Aldershot: Gower).

Thomas, C. (1987) *In Search of Security: The Third World in International Relations* (Brighton: Wheatsheaf).

Thomas, C. (1991) 'New Directions in Thinking about Security in the Third World', in K. Booth (ed.) *New Directions in Strategy and International Security* (London: HarperCollins).

Thomas, C. (ed.) (1994) *Rio: Unravelling the Consequences* (Essex: Frank Cass).

Thomas, C. (1997a) 'Poverty, Development and Hunger', in Baylis, J. and Smith, S. (eds) *Globalization of World Politics* (Oxford: Oxford University Press).

Thomas, C. (1997b) 'Globalization and the South', in C. Thomas and P. Wilkin (eds) *Globalization and the South* (London: Macmillan), pp. 1–17.

Thomas, C. (1998) 'International Financial Institutions and economic and Social Rights: An Exploration', in T. Evans (ed.) *Human Rights Fifty Years On* (Manchester: Manchester University Press).

Thomas, C. (1999a) 'Where is the Third World Now?', *Review of International Studies*, Special Millennium edn, December.

Thomas, C. (1999b) 'Introduction', in C. Thomas and P. Wilkin (eds) *Globalization, Human Security and the African Experience* (Colorado: Lynne Reinner), pp. 1–20.

Thomas, C. and Reader, M. (1997) 'Development and Inequality', in B. White, R. Little and M. Smith (eds) *Issues in Global Politics* (Basingstoke: Macmillan), pp. 90–110.

Thomas, C. and Weber, M. (1999) 'New Values and International Organizations: Balancing Trade and Environment in NAFTA', in A. Taylor and C. Thomas (eds) *Global Trade and Global Social Issues* (London: Routledge).

Thomas, C. and Wilkin, P. (eds) (1997) *Globalization and the South* (London: Macmillan).

Thomas, C. and Wilkin, P. (eds) (1999) *Globalization, Human Security and the African Experience* (Colorado: Lynne Reinner).

Tobin Tax Initiative, USA (2000) 'The Tobin Tax Monthly Update', January <www.tobintax.org>.

Todaro, M. P. (1989) *Economic Development in the Third World* (New York and London: Longman).

Toussaint, E. (1999) *Your Money or Your Life* (London: Pluto Press).

Townsend, P. (1993) *The International Analysis of Poverty* (London: Harvester Wheatsheaf).

TRAC (Transnational Resource and Action Centre) (1999) 'A Perilous Partnership: the UNDP's Flirtation with Corporate Collaboration', posted on <www.corpwatch.org> 12 March.

TUAC (1999) 'The Review of the OECD Guidelines for Multilateral Enterprises', TUAC Briefing Note for Affiliates, December <www.tuac.org/news/nguidelinesrev99e.htm>.

UNCTAD (1998) *Trade and Development Report 1998* (Geneva: UNCTAD).

UNDP (1994) *Human Development Report* (Oxford: Oxford University Press).

UNDP (1996) *Human Development Report* (Oxford: Oxford University Press).

UNDP (1997) *Human Development Report* (Oxford: Oxford University Press).

UNDP (1998) *Human Development Report* (Oxford: Oxford University Press).

UNDP (1999) *Human Development Report* (Oxford: Oxford University Press).

UNICEF (1998) *The State of the World's Children 1998* (New York and Oxford: Oxford University Press).

United Nations Information Services (1999) 'Asian Crisis: Impact Worse than Expected, UN says', <http://www.unfoundation. org>, 8 April.

Vallely, P. (1990) *Bad Samaritans: First World Ethics and Third World Debt* (London: Hodder & Stoughton).

Vidal, J. (2000) 'Wars, famine and lions – how the west views the world', *Guardian*, 28 February, pp. 6–7.

Vivian, J. (ed.) (1995) *Adjustment and Social Sector Restructuring* (Geneva: UNRISD).

Vivian, J. (1995) 'How Safe are Social Safety Nets? Adjustment and Social Sector Restructuring in Developing Countries, in J. Vivian (ed.) *Adjustment and Social Sector Restructuring* (London: Frank Cass, UNRISD).

de Vries, B. (1995) 'The World Bank's focus on poverty', in J. Griesgraber and B. Gunter (eds) *The World Bank: Lending on a Global Scale* (London: Pluto Press), pp. 65–80.

Wallerstein, I. (2000) 'The Head of the IMF: A Secret Radical', *Comment*, 34, 15 February.

Walton, J. and Seddon, D. (1994) *Free Markets and Food Riots: The Politics of Global Adjustment*, (Oxford: Blackwell).

Watkins, K. (1998) *Economic Growth with Equity: Lessons from East Asia* (Oxford: Oxfam).

Watkins, K. (1999) 'Riderless horses and a third world handicap', *Observer*, UK, 18 April.

WCED (1987) *Our Common Future* (*The Brundtland Report*) (Oxford: Oxford University Press).

Weber, H. (2000) *The Politics of Microcredit: Global Governance and Poverty Reduction* (London: Pluto Press).

Wright, M. (1999) 'Doing the Right Thing', *Green Futures*, March/April, pp. 24–8.

Wilkin, P. (1997) 'New Myths for the South: Globalization and the Conflict between Private Power and Freedom', in C. Thomas and P. Wilkin (eds) *Globalization and the South* (London: Macmillan).

Wilkin, P. (2000) 'Solidarity in a Global Age – Seattle and Beyond', paper presented to the International Studies Association Conference, Los Angeles, March 2000. For a copy, contact <p.wilkin@lancaster.ac.uk>.

Wilkinson, R. (1999) 'Labour and trade-related regulation: beyond the trade-labour standards debate?', *British Journal of Politics and International Relations*, 1:2, pp. 165–91.

Williams, M. (1999) 'The WTO Social Movements and "Democracy"', in A. Taylor and C. Thomas (eds) *Global Trade and Global Social Issues* (London: Routledge), pp. 151–70.

Wolf, M. (1999) 'A New Mandate for the IMF: Commentary', *Financial Times*, 15 December.

Wolf, M. (2000) 'Between revolution and reform: The Meltzer Commission's vision for the IMF and World Bank moves in the right direction but is too simplistic', *Financial Times*, 8 March.

Wolfensohn, J. (1999a) 'Proposals for a Comprehensive Development Framework: a discussion draft', 21 January (Washington, DC: World Bank).

Wolfensohn, J. (1999b) Press conference briefing at the beginning of the IMF and World Bank Spring Summit, 22 April (Washington, DC: World Bank).

Wolfensohn, J. (2000) Address to the UN Security Council on HIV/AIDS in Africa, 10 January, World Bank news release 2000/172/S.

Wood, A. (1999) 'Notes on 14th December Treasury Select Committee Meeting for Bretton Woods project' (London: Bretton Woods Project).

Wood, A. and Welch, C. (2000) 'Effective Evaluation at the IMF: How Should an Independent Evaluation Function?', February (London and Washington, DC: Bretton Woods Project and FOE–US).

World Bank (1995) *Mainstreaming the Environment: the World Bank Group and the Environment since the Rio Earth Summit* (Washington, DC: World Bank).

World Bank (1996) *Annual Report 1996* (Washington, DC: World Bank).

World Bank Operations Evaluation Department/Jayarajah, C., Branson, W. and Sen, B. (1996a) *Social Dimensions of Adjustment: World Bank Experience 1980–93* (Washington, DC: World Bank).

World Bank (1997) *World Development Report: the State in a Changing World* (Oxford: Oxford University Press).

World Bank (1999) *Poverty Reduction and the World Bank: Progress in Fiscal 1998* (Washington, DC: World Bank).

World Trade Organization (1999) 'Seattle Preparations Enter New Phase', *WTO Focus*, 37, January–February.

WWF (1998) 'From liberalization to sustainable development' June (Geneva: WWF).

Zadek, S., Pruzan, P. and Evans, R. (eds) (1997) *Building Corporate Accountability: Emerging Practices in Social and Ethical Accounting, Auditing and Reporting* (London: Earthscan).

Index

accountability, 14, 50, 84, 110, 124
acquisitions, 24, 32–3
Action Aid, 36
Adam Smith Institute, 42
ADB, 28, 43, 56
Africa, 5, 56, 88
AFTA, 49
Agenda, 21, 46; agenda-setting, 8, 46
Agreement on Agriculture, 76
agriculture, 47, 70, 71, 76
aid, 10, 14, 82; tied, 83–4
alternative pathway, 22, 94–127
American Express, 66
AMF, 122
Amnesty International, 87
Anglo-Saxon, 33, 71
Angola, 43
anti-racist movements, 50
APEC, 49, 73
aquaculture, 48
AsDB, 43, 66
ASEAN, 49
Asia, 28, 86
AT&T, 115
AT&T/TCI, 33
Australia, 49, 86
Axworthy, L., 6

Bangalore, 29
Bangladesh, 66
Bank America, 79
Bankhaus Herstatt, 81
base ecclesiastical communities, 36
basic needs, 37, 44
Basle Capital Accord, 81
Basle Committee, 79

BBC2, 10
Beijing Conference, 16
Belgium, 81
Bell Atlantic/GTE, 33
Berlin Wall, 41
billionaires, 24, 28
biotechnology, 32, 73
BIS, 15, 18
Blair, Tony, 108
blueprint, 13, 17, 36, 79
Bolivia, 63
bond-rating agency, 15
BP, 88
BP/Amoco, 33
Brazil, 20, 27, 30, 37, 50, 64, 79, 93 102
Bretton Woods Project, 125
broadcasting, 90, 10
broken promises, 81–2
Brunei, 121
Burma, 108
Burundi, 118
Bush, George, 36, 74

CAFOD, 36
Cairo, 16
Camdessus, 3, 8, 17, 20, 55, 62, 64, 76, 93, 103, 124
Campaign against Hunger, 36
Canada, 6, 19, 49, 66, 73–5, 80, 86, 122, 124
capital: controls, 120, 121; markets, 77; mobility, 4; movements, 122; speculative, 120
capitalism, 11, 14
Caribbean, 28
Cartels, 70
caste, 7

center of Concern, 125
Central Europe, 26, 89
central planning, 35
CERDS, 114, 115
CGAP, 66, 67
Channel 4, 10
charities, 10
Chase Manhattan, 66
Chiapas, 32, 48
child labour, 88
children, 12, 31
Chile, 89, 115, 120
China, 27, 30, 50, 66–7, 102
Christian Aid, 36
Chrysler, 32, 33
CIS, 25, 26, 27
Citicorp, 66
Citizen Agenda, 115
citizen submission process, 75
civil society, 14, 50, 64, 96, 111,
    123
civil wars, 43
class, 61
Clean Clothes Campaign, 87
Clinton, Bill, 74
codes of conduct, 104, 106, 115
coffee, 118, 119
Cold War, 6, 41
collectives, 119
Colombia, 88
commodities, 70, 72
commons, 31, 48
communism, 13, 88, 110
communist bloc, 10, 11, 36
competition policy, 97
computers, 32
conflicts, 9
Congress, 74
conservation, 75
contagion effect, 79
Co-op, 119
Copenhagen, 7, 50
core: standards, 115; values,
    94–6, 112–14; workforce, 27–9
corporate: accountability, 103–9,
    114–16, 127; responsibility, 88;
    rights 85, 87
cosmetics, 127
counter-hegemony, 14
credit, 57, 66–67, 117, 118, 119

crony capitalism, 80
cross-retaliation, 72
culture: diversity, 112; specificity,
    47
currency: regime, 121;
    speculation, 120; trading, 79
Czech Republic, 21

DAC, 43, 82, 83
Dag Hammarskjold Foundation,
    37
Daimler, 32, 33
Darwinism, 40
debt, 45, 46, 56, 63–4, 82
democracy, 6, 7, 21, 41, 43, 44,
    52; movements, 36;
    substantive, 112
development; agenda, 3, 4;
    alternative, 5, 34–52; ideas,
    34–52; market-led, 55–68;
    model, 17, 34–52, 93;
    neoliberal, 5, 93–109, 112;
    orthodoxy, 34–46; policy, 5, 7,
    9, 14, 21, 22, 34–52, 114, 126;
    state-led, 55; sustainable, 14,
    37, 82
digital divide, 29
Dinka, 88
dispute settlement, 72
distribution, 37, 59, 62, 109

Earth Summit, 16
East, 116
East Asia, 20, 25, 27, 29, 36, 56,
    67, 78, 79, 93, 121
Eastern bloc, 35, 41, 81
Eastern Europe, 25, 26, 27, 36,
    89
EBRD, 43, 84
EBNSC, 104
ECAs, 77, 83–4
ECLAC, 89
ecology, 14, 111
e-commerce, 28, 29
economic: genocide, 60; protec-
    tionism, 35; restructuring 20,
    32, 55–68, 89; sovereignty, 17,
    70, 87, 115
economy-capitalist world, 7;
    subsistence, 34

education, 12, 35, 39, 65, 82, 127
Egypt, 50, 60
electronics, 72, 89
embedded liberalism, 4, 35, 42, 45, 111
emerging markets, 78, 83
employment laws, 30
empowerment, 44, 46–51, 67, 112
entitlement, 7, 39, 52, 57
environment, 3, 12, 106; issues, 74–5; movements, 50, 70, 111; standards, 31, 70, 84, 117; and trade, 73–5
ESA, 74–5
ESAF, 56, 63–4
ESCAP, 26, 28
ESF, 63
ethical trade, 117, 119–20; initiatives, 119
ethnicity, 7
EU, 71, 103, 122
Europe, 19, 124, 127
exclusion, 30, 31, 32
exit tax, 121
expert knowledge, 34
export agriculture, 47
export processing zone, 30
Exxon, 32, 33

Fairtrade, 116–20; Foundation, 117; Mark, 117; Register, 118
farmers' organisations, 118
fast-track, 74
Federal Reserve Bank, 81
feminisation, 30
finance, 13, 14, 111, 120–3, 126; national regulation of, 120–1; private, 77–81; public, 81–4
financial: crisis, 26, 27, 93, 94, 110; deregulation, 80; liberalisation, 56, 69, 76–84, 90, 99–103; markets, 121; services, 72
Finland, 122
First World, 10, 23, 25, 26, 111, 115, 125
First World War, 9
flexible labour practices, 30
floriculture, 48

food security, 73, 75–76
Ford, 30
Ford Foundation, 66
foreign direct investment, 24, 25, 30, 32, 44, 84–90, 114–16
France, 19, 66, 80, 122
free trade agreements, 70
Freedom from Debt Coalition, 36
free market beliefs, 40–1
Friedman, Milton, 41
Fukuyama, Francis, 41

garment industry, 30
GATT, 18, 69, 71
GDOs, 36–7
GDP, 19, 27, 28, 85, 103
gender, 7, 50, 61, 82, 111
Germany, 19, 27, 80, 122
Ghana, 65
Global Compact, 104–7, 116
global governance, 3, 4, 5, 7, 8, 9, 13, 14, 17, 18, 19, 21, 22, 23, 25, 26, 33, 34–6, 50, 55–68, 93, 96, 109, 111, 112, 123–7
GNP, 24, 25
government procurement, 97
Grameen Bank, 66
greenfield investment, 32
green movements, 36
green revolution, 58
Green Room meetings, 124
Greenspan, Alan, 102, 123
growth: equity, 25, 39, 57, 61; export-led, 4
G7, 17, 18, 21, 42, 43, 46, 77, 84, 94, 103
G8, 17
G10, 81
G20, 102, 103
G11, 19
G77, 19, 115, 126

Harker report, 88
harmonisation, 75
HDI, 8, 50, 51
health, 3, 12, 35
hedge funds, 20, 78, 80, 81
hegemony, 13, 21, 47
Heritage Foundation, 42
HIPC, 63–4

HIV/AIDS, 3, 12, 73
Hoechst, 32
horticulture, 48
households, 7, 119
House of Commons, 83
human: capital, 63; -centred
    development, 124; dignity,
    112; needs, 113, 122; poverty,
    6, 25, 113; poverty index, 30;
    rights, 103–9; security, 4, 5–9,
    21, 29; 110–27
Human Rights Watch, 87
Human Settlements, 16
Hungary, 21

ICC, 15
ice-cream, 127
ICFTU, 49, 104
IFC, 29, 77, 84
illiteracy, 31
ILO, 17, 30, 66
IMF, 3, 8, 13, 15, 17, 21, 34, 36,
    39, 42, 43, 47, 55–68, 93, 94,
    100–2, 109, 121, 122, 125;
    evaluation unit, 125
income, 8, 23, 24, 25; poverty, 6,
    7, 25, 113
index-linking, 70
India, 47, 51, 73, 102, 120
indigenous communities, 32
Indonesia, 26, 125
inequality, 3, 5, 8, 9, 10, 13, 14,
    21, 22–33
informal sector, 4
information technology, 72–3
intellectual property rights, 48
internet, 24, 28, 29
interwar period, 35
investment, 13, 111, 114–16, 126;
    agreements, 85–7, 104;
    bankers, 39; concerns, 87–90;
    and human rights, 87–8; liber-
    alisation, 69, 84–90, 103–9;
    policy, 97; regulation, 114–16
invisible hand, 97
IOSCO, 18
ISI, 35
ISO, 107–8; ISO 9000, 107
Istanbul, 16
Italy, 27, 80

ITV, 9
IUCN, 44

Japan, 19, 80, 86, 124, 127
job creation, 30, 32
job losses, 32
Jubilee 2000, 61, 63–4

Karnataka, 47
Keynes, Maynard, 35, 41
knowledge, 14, 37

labour: capacity, 29; cost, 27;
    groups, 71, 74; issues, 73–5;
    laws, 49, 56; market, 26, 30;
    standards, 31, 70, 75, 106,
    116–17
landless, 32
land reform, 48
land tenure, 9
Latin America, 29, 30, 36, 49, 56,
    78, 79, 86, 88
law, 14
legitimacy, 15, 33, 44–6, 52
liberalisation, 21, 30, 39, 40, 67,
    68–90, 111, 114
liberal-pluralists, 9
literacy, 50
local purchasing power, 50
Lome, 72
LTCM, 26, 79, 81

MAI, 21, 86–7, 105, 108
Mahatir, Mohammed, 120, 121
Malaysia, 45, 50, 111, 120
marginalisation, 14
marginalised workforce, 31–2
media, 10, 46
Meltzer commission, 100–1
Mendes, Chico, 37
Mergers, 24, 32–3
Mexico, 21, 31, 48, 50, 73–5, 89
microcredit, 66–7, 68; summit,
    66
microfinance, 66, 67, 68, 119
MIGA, 84
Millennium Challenge, 104
Mobil, 32, 33
monetary policy, 122
Monsanto, 46

moral hazard, 80, 81
migration, 30
military spending, 127
mortality, 11, 82
Mozambique, 67
multilateral development, 13, 37, 55

NAAEC, 74–5
NAFTA 32, 69, 70, 73–5, 98
national: economic reform, 13, 55–68; security, 35, 90; strategy document, 64
Nations Bank/Bank America, 33
neoclassical economic theory, 36, 39–42
neoliberal: development, 13–15, 16, 38, 39–46; ideology, 14, 16, 46, 55–68
Nestlé, 107
Netherlands, 66, 80
New Zealand, 90
NGOs, 36–7, 47, 50, 72, 112, 115
Nicaragua, 118
NIEO, 115
Nigeria, 50
non-western, 9
North 11, 34, 116, 126
North America, 28
Northwest/Wells Fargo, 33
nutrition, 12

ODA, 81
ODI, 65
OECD, 18, 20, 21, 24, 27, 43, 59, 81, 82, 83, 86, 105, 108
offsetting measures, 98
offshore banking, 78
Ogoni, 86
Oxfam, 36, 63, 88

PAMSCAD, 65
participation, 37, 38, 46–51, 111
partnerships, 104–7
patents, 24, 73
peace: dividend, 11, 81; movement, 36, 50, 111
Peru, 30
pesticides, 24

pet foods, 127
Philippines, 37
Poland, 19, 21, 26, 120
polarisation, 4, 22–33, 110; corporate, 32–3; interstate, 23–6; intrastate, 26–32
political: liberalisation, 43, 44; science, 10
population, 8, 10, 11, 15, 16, 19, 24, 25, 30
portfolio flows, 77
post-Cold War, 9
post-industrialist, 9
poverty, 3, 4, 5, 8, 9, 13, 23–3, 57–67, 110, 112; line, 27; reduction, 64–7
power: private, 6, 13; social, 123; structures, 4, 6, 9, 14, 124
precarious workforce, 29–31
precautionary approach, 106
Premier Oil, 108
PRGF, 56, 63–4
prison labour, 88
private: finance, 77–81; flows, 78; regulation, 108
privatisation, 32, 39, 40, 48, 89
producers, 27–32
property rights, 6, 40, 110
protest, 14, 47–52, 112
public: enforcement agency, 95; finance, 81, 84; goods, 15, 16; realm, 13; regulation, 104, 115, 123; sphere, 113

race, 50, 61, 111
Reagan, Ronald, 36, 42
redistribution, 48, 95, 110–27
reformers, 57–60
reformist pathway, 22, 93–109
refugees, 16
regional action, 120, 121–2
regulation: TNCs, 45, 50
regulatory frameworks, 77
religion, 7
rent-seeking, 99
representation, 102–3, 112
reproductive rights, 127
resistance, 46–52
RFSTNRP, 48
Rhône-Poulenc, 32

Rio, 16, 45
risk, 23, 27, 30, 60, 77, 79, 93
Roman Catholic Church, 36
Rome Food Summit, 16
rubber-tappers, 36
rule-based, 71–2, 75, 95
Russia, 20, 26, 79, 89, 93, 102, 125
Russian Federation, 19, 27
Rwanda, 43

SADC, 74
SAPs, 21, 56–68, 75
Saudi Arabia, 19
Save the Children Fund, 36
SBA/Ameritech, 33
Seattle, 14, 49, 112, 126
Second World, 11, 15
Second World War, 4, 35
security: agenda, 3; orthodoxy, 5
self-regulation, 105, 115
self-reliance, 37, 38, 116
self-sufficiency, 37, 38, 116
Shiva, Vandana, 48
Sierra Leone, 43
socialism, 10, 52
socialist countries, 35
social labelling, 106
Social Safety Nets, 62–3, 67
South, 11, 34, 116, 126
South Africa, 51, 73
South Asia, 25
South East Asia, 29, 44, 49
South Korea, 20, 30, 49, 76
sovereignty, 122
Spencer, Herbert, 40
spending, military, 11
stakeholders, 105
state: -assisted capitalism, 49; capacity, 9, 44; collapse, 9; legitimacy, 9; society relations, 10
Stock Exchange, 33
structural adjustment, 45, 46, 55; impact, 57–61
Sub-Saharan Africa, 29, 31, 36, 78
subsides, 57, 60, 95
Sudan, 43
Summers, Lawrence, 100–1

super-rich, 28
supervision of finance, 77, 80–1
Sweden, 27, 46, 80, 115
Switzerland, 80, 122

Talisman, 88
Tanzania, 118
technical co-operation, 83
technology, 3, 10, 11, 13, 28, 34, 35, 37, 48, 106
telecommunications, 24, 32, 90
telephone lines, 25, 28, 29
textiles, 71
Thatcher, Margaret, 14, 36, 42
Third World: 11, 15, 23–33, 49, 86, 111, 116, 125; Network, 36, 111
TINA, 13
TNBs, 90, 94
TNCs, 13, 15, 30, 46, 70, 72, 73, 75, 84–90, 94, 115, 116
Tobin Tax, 120, 122–3
Trade, 13, 14, 24, 96–9, 111, 116–20, 125, 126; liberalisation, 30, 56, 69–76, 90, 96–9
transformers, 60–1
transitional countries, 19, 23
transparency, 14, 50, 84, 124
Travellers/Citicorp, 33
tribal people, 36
trickle down, 11, 25, 38, 58, 94, 95
TRIMS, 71–3, 86
TRIPS, 71–3
trust, 20, 81–2, 113
Turkey, 21, 50

Uganda, 63, 118
UK, 19, 27, 30, 42, 80, 90; Treasury Select Committee, 125
Ukraine, 30
Ul Haq, Mahbub, 7
UN, 3, 4
UNCED, 16, 44–6, 115
UN Commission on Human Rights, 87
UN Conferences, 16, 44–6, 82
UNCTAD, 3, 17, 18, 70, 76, 120
UNCTC, 46, 115

UNDP, 11, 16, 17, 29, 50, 66
unemployment, 26, 28, 30, 35, 109
UNICEF, 58, 59, 62, 65
UNRATTI, 116
UN Secretary General, 103, 104–7
UN Security Council, 3
Uruguay Round, 70, 71, 73, 86
US, 19, 27, 42, 46, 49, 50, 71, 73–5, 80, 86, 124, 127; Treasury, 124

veto, 124
voluntary; actions, 104; guidelines, 108; initiatives, 104
von Hayek, F. A., 41
voting, 19, 72

Wall Street, 124; -Treasury complex, 94
war 9
Washington consensus, 34, 39–46, 94, 96, 109, 111
Water, 11

WBCSD, 104
WCED, 44
Weber, Max, 67
welfare state, 35, 42
WES, 15, 104
West, 116
Western bloc, 35; norms, 13; Europe, 28
WHO, 104
wildlife, 10
WIPO, 72
woman, 12, 66–8
women's movement, 36, 111
World Bank, 3, 8, 13, 15, 17, 18, 21, 34, 36, 39, 42, 43, 46, 50, 55–68, 94
World Summit on Social Development, 7, 44
World Vision, 36
WTO, 13, 14, 15, 17, 18, 49, 69–73, 76, 86, 94, 104, 123, 125, 126

Zeneca/Astra 33